D1433715

The Kiss

The Kiss

THE STORY OF AN OBSESSION

HUGO VICKERS

HAMISH HAMILTON · LONDON

HAMISH HAMILTON LTD

Published by the Penguin Group
Penguin Books Ltd, 27 Wrights Lane, London w8 5tz, England
Penguin Books USA Inc., 375 Hudson Street, New York, New York 10014, USA
Penguin Books Australia Ltd, Ringwood, Victoria, Australia
Penguin Books Canada Ltd, 10 Alcorn Avenue, Toronto, Ontario, Canada m4v 3b2
Penguin Books (NZ) Ltd, 182–190 Wairau Road, Auckland 10, New Zealand

Penguin Books Ltd, Registered Offices: Harmondsworth, Middlesex, England

First published 1996
3 5 7 9 10 8 6 4 2

Set in 10.5/13pt Monotype Baskerville
Typeset by RefineCatch Limited, Bungay, Suffolk
Printed in England by Clays Ltd, St Ives plc

A CIP catalogue record for this book is available from the British Library

ISBN 0 241 12711 4

To Mouse
With my love

Contents

Part Three

Illustrations

Acknowledgements

I began to write this book as long ago as 1988 and it has taken me a long time to bring it to conclusion. The book could not have been written but for the original friendship of Joan and Christian Kappey, and also that of Dick Bonham. I must also mention the kindness of the Rev. J. W. Crane, then Minor Canon of St George's Chapel, Windsor, who arranged my first meeting with Major H. K. Clough and thus with the two sisters.

I am especially grateful for the kindness of Major John and Hon. Mrs Bonham, who received me in Ireland and talked to me of some of the events in this book. Major Bonham has kindly allowed me to quote some letters written by his brother both to Joan Kappey and to me.

Major and Mrs Charles Hamilton entertained me at Hamwood and showed me Hamilton family albums. I am also grateful to the Hon. Desmond Guinness for his encouragement, and to Dominick Hamilton. Mairi de Courcy O'Grady kindly talked to me of the friendship she and her late husband, Patrick, enjoyed with Dick Bonham, and read the book in typescript, saving me from perpetuating several errors. Through her I was able to talk to Mrs Dawn Wood, and her mother, Mrs Charles Keeler, both of whom added to the story.

On the Kappey side, I am grateful to Miss Betty Worthington for talking to me about her friends, the two Miss Kappeys, and also for recalling events in the story which went back many years. Mrs Geoffrey Bourne-May has kindly allowed me to quote her late husband's letter and furthermore recalled her own memories of the Kappeys. Joan's cousin, Mrs Michael Arnison-Newgass, filled in details of her side of the family. Mr and Mrs Michael Antony, the present owners of Dargai, kindly permitted me to return to the house that holds so many memories.

I am grateful to Alec D'Janoeff for reviving some memories of the Military Knights of Windsor in the late 1960s, Philip Hoare for his encouragement and for reading part of the manuscript in its early stages, and to Verena Vickers for forging a vital link. My aunt, Joyce Caruana, described the area of South Africa where Reggie Kappey spent his last days. The Mother-in-Charge at Iden Manor in Kent kindly spoke to me of Mrs Kathleen Kappey, who resided there for many years. I received considerable help from Mrs Irene Clark, a colleague of the late Denys Graves at Stratford.

There were many whose advice and help I sought: Earl and Countess Granville, Mr Douglas Brodie Good, Mrs A. A. Crook, Mrs Denis Howard, Miss Diana Hughes-Hughes, Miss Mary Kerridge, Mrs Vilma King, Mr Patrick Manley, Mr Hedley Mattingley, Benda, Lady Milverton, Mrs R. L. Penfold, Mr Randal Sadleir, Mr Graham Sawyer, Mrs Christiane Sherwen, Miss Nora Swinburne, Mr Rodney Tye, and my mother-in-law, Mrs Michael Vickers (who also kindly checked the proofs).

Louise Corrigan helped me in the early stages and recalls that when the Kappey papers first arrived in the office in London, they were accompanied by odours that testified to Joan Kappey's devotion to a number of elderly cats. Latterly I received constructive advice on the text from my wife, to whom this book is dedicated, and also her brother Edmund.

I wish to apologize to any copyright-holders that may have eluded detection. Due acknowledgement will be made in any subsequent edition.

This book was originally commissioned by Christopher Sinclair-Stevenson when he was in charge of Hamish Hamilton. I recall with pleasure its inception in discussion with him and my agent, Gillon Aitken, over lunch in the Launceston Place Restaurant. It is now published under the aegis of Clare Alexander.

I have been particularly fortunate that it has been edited by Charles Drazin, whose insight has been wholly constructive, encouraging and supportive. He succeeded in getting me to undertake a lot of extra work, but in such a way that I greatly enjoyed doing it – a unique experience.

Hugo Vickers
Wyeford, June 1996

Family Trees of the
Kappey and Mills Families

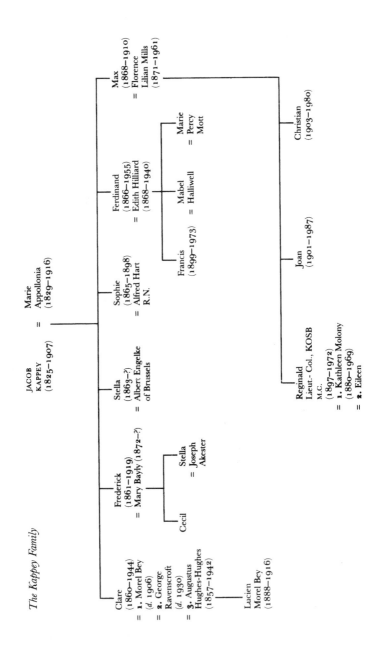

The Kappey Family

JACOB KAPPEY (1825–1907) = Marie Appollonia (1829–1916)

Clare (1860–1944)
= 1. Morel Bey (d. 1906)
= 2. George Ravenscroft (d. 1930)
= 3. Augustus Hughes-Hughes (1857–1942)

Lucien Morel Bey (1888–1916)

Frederick (1861–1919) = Mary Bayly (1872–?)

Cecil

Stella = Joseph Akester

Stella (1863–?) = Albert Engelke of Brussels

Sophie (1865–1898) = Alfred Hart R.N.

Francis (1899–1973)

Mabel = Halliwell

Ferdinand (1866–1955) = Edith Hilliard (1868–1940)

Marie = Percy Mott

Max (1868–1910) = Florence Lilian Mills (1871–1961)

Reginald Lieut.- Col., KOSB M.C. (1897–1972)
= 1. Kathleen Molony (1880–1969)
= 2. Eileen

Joan (1901–1987)

Christian (1903–1980)

The Mills Family

JOHN MILLS
of Hastings

George Jonathan (1820–1903)
= 1. Jane (1821–1872) = 2. Georgiana (1847–1913)

George Jonathan (1845–1939)
= Jane Weston (1848–1925)

Georgiana = Tanner

Jean (1878–1958)
= 1. White Maconochie, MP (1855–1926)
= 2. Montague Pitkin

William (Canon)

Robert (1885–1963) = Florence

Frank (Rev.)

James (Rev.) (1891–1950)

William (1869–1876)

Florence Lilian (1871–1961)
= Major Max Kappery (1868–1910)

Arthur (1873–1951) m. twice

George Jonathan (1868–19?)

Dorothy = Professor George Brown

Kathleen = A. Harper

Margaret OBE (1874–1960)
= 1. Rev. T. Stanley
= 2. John Titley

Stuart (1876–1969)

Jean (1877–1958)
= Col. Walter East (1853–1929)

Marjorie
= 1. H.J. Stewart Murray
= 2. Rosser-Dummer

Vera = Stanley de Freitas

Sylvia = Charles Miles

Geoffrey (1904–1988)
= Coralie Swinburne (d. 1989)

Audrey (1906–1991)
= J.P. Long (1907–1941)

Virginia (b. 1939)
= Michael Arnison-Newgass

Part One

I

The Kiss

This story has taken some strange twists over the years. It is a true story in which all the protagonists are now dead. It concerns two spinster sisters who lived together in a dilapidated Victorian house in Windsor, and a man who lived in an equally strange house not far away. I knew the two spinsters and I visited their home. Their house was shrouded in sadness. Family life continued there after a fashion for the survivors. The original occupants had gone. Yet though they were gone, the house was left as if they might return. The house wore many aspects of a shrine, with old family photographs in silver frames in every corner. But there was a more powerful image. There was a haunting photograph of the man, staring into the room from every wall and corner, his image multiplied so that he could not be escaped.

At that time I did not know who he was, why he was there or even if he was alive or dead. Later I learned that he lived in the other strange house. I heard part of his story, and later still I was able to unravel the complicated circumstances which led to his conversion into an icon.

This story leads up to one date, 22 December 1960. It goes back almost a hundred years and it goes forward to the end. On that fateful December day, there was a kiss, which changed two lives. For one it was a consecration; for the other, the beginning of a long, unending persecution. 22 December

1960 was the day of the kiss. 'Thank God – my darling Dick came this morn and brought his Christmas gifts, bless him. Heavenly seeing him. He is so *adorable* – and gave me the most wonderful kiss I have ever had in my life – blessed darling.'

In 1966, the spinster who had been kissed wrote to remind the man of that day:

My adored Dick

Exactly six years ago, *this Thursday* Dec. 22nd – *your dear lips met mine* – in that *blessed & wonderful kiss* ever there and sacred – for it awoke *my very soul Dick* – and made *you mine* and *me yours* in *my heart*, as long as I live, whatever happens. No one has kissed them since – or ever will *Dicky* – as long as I remain conscious. I told you this once before and I repeat it – and mean every *word* I say Dick. *Please* believe this – in the sight of God – As ever at Christmas, & as the New Year dawns – and every day of the years to come, my Heart will be *with you, close to yours* my Beloved Dick, as I love & *trust* you till you make it real . . .

This story took place in Windsor and Ascot, though its participants came there from far and wide, and travelled widely. There came to rest, in that Windsor house, souvenirs of Turkey and France and India. Letters arrived from every corner of the globe and none were thrown away. Yet despite these links across the world, the house's occupants were resolutely parochial.

Windsor is dominated by its castle, and its strong royal connections. For most of those who live in the Windsor area, the knowledge that the castle is the Queen's dwelling is of supreme importance. For the people of this story, the Queen was the focal point. They did not meet her, but they saw her often – at events such as the Garter ceremony, the Windsor Horse Show, and the polo at Smith's Lawn. They admired and loved her and would have supported and defended her to their last breath.

There are many strata of life in and around Windsor, from the old Windsor families to the military, to the itinerant population that satellite around the Sovereign. Smith's Lawn itself is a kind of microcosm, attracting a disparate crowd of corporate sponsors, dashing South American polo-players, young men in blazers and smart girls drifting. The people of whom I write were there too, the two spinster sisters and their group of friends. But they were not in the smart stands, entry to which was above their means. You may have seen them, perched on metal chairs and shooting-sticks, or seated on old Scottish tartan rugs, wearing drab clothes and hats like tea-cosies, pouring tea from old thermoses, and gathered round old grey Austins. They were easy to ignore, and yet under these unpromising exteriors lurked much accumulated experience, love and suffering.

They could be called indigent gentlefolk but the description overlooks their inherent dignity, pride and independence. And they all had their connections. They lived almost in the shadow of Windsor Castle, and went there often, being on the fringe of one of the many communities that dwelt within its walls. Their particular friends were the Military Knights of Windsor. Of 'all the Queen's men', they were the ones they knew best.

It was the elder of the two spinster sisters who was kissed by the man in the photograph. The other sister was in love with the oldest surviving Military Knight. He was called Major H. K. Clough. For me, meeting him was the key that unlocked the door to this extraordinary world.

2

Major Clough and the Military Knights of Windsor

I was aware of Major Clough some three years before I met him. My first sighting of him was on the day the Queen came to open St George's House in October 1966. Henry ('Billy') Clough was the senior Military Knight. Born in December 1876, he was approaching his ninetieth birthday. He still marched in every Sunday, gallantly upright, if a little bandy of leg. A widower, he was deeply religious and also attended early communion and evensong. He once turned to a 'new boy' amongst the Military Knights, a Colonel with a magnificent handlebar moustache, and told him: 'I am the senior Knight. I don't recommend it. There's not much future in it, I'm afraid.' Once at the funeral of another Military Knight, he could be heard by his colleagues saying, 'I'll be the next to go,' a theme he expanded upon during the remainder of the service.

A photograph survives of the opening of St George's House in which the Dean and the Sovereign are walking past the line-up of the Military Knights. Major Clough appears in the background. For his ninetieth birthday the Queen signed a copy of it and it was proudly displayed in his house. He was also immortalized in the late Terence Cuneo's depiction of the 1964 Garter ceremony, which now hangs in the Chapter Library. He lived at number 7 Lower Ward from 1935 to 1970.

The son of a clergyman and a descendant of the Delves-

6

Broughton family, Billy Clough had begun life in an imposing Regency-built rectory with eleven bedrooms and a three-acre garden at Clifton with Glapton in Nottinghamshire. As a boy of sixteen, he enjoyed nothing more than to join his slightly younger friend, Christopher ('Toddy') Hodgson, the son of the Rector of neighbouring Barton-in-Fabis, for a day's fishing on the River Trent. They would set off, well supplied with fishing tackle and a flower-pot of worms to use as bait. They fished with cherry-wood rods about four feet long, purchased for twopence in the nearest town, four miles away. They walked there and back to get them. In some triumph one day, Billy caught a giant bream weighing 2lbs 2oz., but when it was cooked for him it tasted revolting.

In his youth Major Clough served in the King's Own Lancaster Regiment. He saw action in the South African War, including operations in Natal in 1900 and at Laing's Neck, and later for two years he was in the Transvaal. He was a Marshal in the King's Procession at Caernarvon Castle during the Investiture of the Prince of Wales (later Duke of Windsor) in 1911, and in advance of Prince Charles's Investiture in 1969, officials came to ask him what he remembered. He wrote to the Duke of Windsor to tell him he had been there and received a long typed reply, signed by the Duke.

The Major also served in the Great War and was awarded the OBE. He was passionately interested in uniforms and at one time compiled a register of cavalry and yeomanry officers' full-dress uniforms as worn in Queen Victoria's reign and up to the First World War. He collected all the Simkin prints. For some years he lived in a cottage at Westbrook in Berkshire before coming to Windsor.

His prime reason for coming to Windsor was that his childhood fishing friend and fellow officer, Colonel Hodgson, had been appointed a Military Knight in 1932. The link of their lifelong friendship had been further strengthened when, in 1904, Billy Clough married Toddy Hodgson's sister, Grace. Indeed it was strengthened further when Toddy married Billy's sister. Grace Clough was unusual among the wives of the Military Knights. She could be spotted in her garden smoking a clay pipe. She died in 1958, but for thirty years the two brother officers were near neighbours in the Lower Ward.

The Military Knights of Windsor dwell in houses built in the walls of Windsor Castle. Every Sunday at about 10.30 a.m. they come out and walk slowly across to St George's Chapel for morning service. Tourists are already milling about aimlessly and are naturally confused when they see in their midst these distinguished old gentlemen in uniforms designed in the days of King William IV. The Knights are dressed in scarlet, the uniform of an unattached officer or officer on half-pay as worn in 1834. The uniform consists of a tail-coat, buttoned to the neck, worn with gold epaulettes and a white shoulder-belt. The hat is topped with plumes, a white plume emerging from a red one. The Knights are retired officers, Brigadiers, Colonels and Majors.

Formerly known as 'the Poor Knights', they must possess less than a certain capital sum, and in olden times if they inherited or acquired more than that sum they were obliged to resign. There are thirteen Military Knights in all and it is usually a life appointment. Joining in their late fifties, they become gradually decrepit as they gallantly fight off the effects of old age after a life of distinguished service. It sounds unchivalrous to describe them thus, but it is the way they have in the past described themselves. In 1643 they petitioned King Charles I for moneys unpaid and owing. The appeal came from 'so many old decayed Gentlemen who have spent the best part of our lives in the service of our country'. In the 1960s their annual stipend was £56, hardly a lavish sum.

The principal duty of the Military Knights is to attend Chapel every Sunday on behalf of the Knights of the Garter, who have always been too worldly to attend mattins at St George's on a regular basis. They also march in the annual Garter procession. At the funeral of the Earl of Athlone on a cold day in January 1957, they lined the west steps of the Chapel, wearing their full-dress uniforms under black military cloaks, rather in the style of Sherlock Holmes. Some of today's Knights lined the Grand Entrance Hall when President Gorbachev arrived to lunch with the Queen in April 1989. They occasionally travel as a body to London to be on duty at a Coronation or a royal wedding, but Windsor remains their home and their precinct.

On fine summer mornings they create a colourful spectacle as they approach the Chapel in ones or twos. In the winter they normally wear a blue frock-coat undress uniform, and there are misty photographs of the old men making their way across. When they arrive at St George's their fine old military voices can be heard booming and chatting until their Governor, a Major-General,* brings them to line in the ambulatory and addresses them briefly.

'I have been to see Tommy Smith in the Edward VII and his leg is making good progress. He hopes to be back home at the end of the week. As you know, I interviewed a Major Craig but he has now decided not to join us for personal reasons, and I shall be seeing a new candidate next week. We are expected to turn out on Thursday, full-dress uniform, for the presentation of Lord Rhodes's Garter banner at evensong. Mourning bands to be worn.

---

* When I was at school, the Governor of the Military Knights was Major-General Sir Edmund Hakewill Smith, a portly figure who moved with slow dignity and spoke with a hollow voice that seemed to come from the pit of his stomach. He retired in 1978 and died at Hampton Court Palace in 1986.

'Military Knights, right and left turn. To the nave, advance.'

Then the old men stomp off as it seems they must have done since time immemorial, but in fact it is only since 1927 that they have been granted the privilege of marching to their seats in the Nave or Quire. The most recently appointed lead the procession and the senior Knight brings up the rear. He in turn is followed by the General.

Throughout their history Military Knights have always appeared exceptionally old. Russell Thorndike, brother of Dame Sybil, was a chorister at St George's Chapel in the last years of Queen Victoria. He remembered 'some half-dozen old and distinguished-looking officers in long military coats' seated in the front row of the Quire, with their cocked hats on ledges behind their hassocks.

One old knight, a survivor of the Crimean War, used to recite 'The Charge of the Light Brigade' with great spirit, and add that he considered the poem as fine as the charge itself. Most popular with the boys then was Colonel Francis Maude (1828–1900), who had won the Victoria Cross in the Indian Mutiny. 'We were always thrilled to hear him recount what he had seen with his own eyes,' wrote Thorndike.

At one time I knew all the Military Knights, some of them quite well. I would not have been surprised if one of them had told me a story of the Crimean War. Sadly the passage of time means that all my old friends are now in ashes interred under stones in the floor of the Dean's Cloister. The ones I knew as a teenager seemed to come from another age, adorned as they were with handlebar moustaches, and medals won in the First World War and earlier. The last Knight to have served in the First World War died in 1982. Today's Knights look younger and less awesome than their predecessors. Recently a friend commented: 'It is one thing when policemen look young. But when Military Knights begin to look young, you really feel old!'

Military Knights tend to be fairly conservative in their attitudes. The only time they ever disappointed me was when they all appeared at the Garter Ceremony of 1976. For some years prior to this a number of them had announced to friends, 'I shan't turn out if that fellow Wilson is made a Garter Knight.' Yet there they were, inevitably, on parade when Sir Harold walked down the hill.

The first Military Knight I met was Billy Clough's friend and brother-in-law, Colonel Hodgson. He had been secretary of the Cresta Run in St Moritz, down which perilous descent my father had sped in his youth, and he was an old friend of my family. Toddy Hodgson had been a great character. One of the stories told of him was that he liked to fish at Frogmore. However, he was briefly banned from the river because Queen Mary heard him swearing when his endeavours were not crowned with success. In old age he travelled about in a tiny wheelchair, always in danger of toppling over, as his weight, the centre of gravity, was outside the chair.

When I went to Eton my father suggested I should ring the Colonel up. I did so, and his wife invited me to tea. When I arrived, by an agonizing misunderstanding I was told that my mother had telephoned and that she was coming. Much of the time was spent looking out for her until the confusion was resolved. They had mistaken my call for hers. It was an awkward occasion.

It was from the roof of Colonel Hodgson's house that I witnessed my first Garter Ceremony in June 1965 and I have never missed one since. The following November the Colonel died, aged eighty-six, and I attended my first funeral.

Amongst the other Military Knights, there were some magnificent characters. There was Brigadier Crook, who was very lame, and when asked how he was would reply with unfailing regularity: 'My old rugby knee playing me up again.' Towards the end of his life he was too lame to march down the hill in the Garter procession, so he joined his fellow Knights at the Great West Door. On the way out he said, in his version of a stage whisper, 'Well done, old boy!' to the Knight marching beside him. His voice boomed out above the organ voluntary. Having gained a certain momentum on the way down the aisle there was no stopping him. He was set to retrieve his place at the Great West Door, and a line of Household Cavalry state trumpeters parted with undignified rapidity and a quest for self-preservation in order to let him through.

Another Knight, Brigadier Robinson, sported a black moustache and a mouth which turned down at each side and appeared so fiercely and rigidly shut that you would never have believed it could open again. In uniform he was a terrifying figure, and a friend of mine who was in the choir in the early 1960s recalled receiving a sharp clip over the head from him for being late putting out the music and being still about his work as the Knights marched in. Out of uniform, the Brigadier was a charming man. He broadcast regularly on *Woman's Hour* about his experiences as a child in London at the turn of the century, recalling the clip-clop of the hansom cab over the cobbled streets outside his house. After tea he would suggest that his young guests might like to 'wash their hands'. When we declined in unison, he commented, 'You must have strong bladders!'

In the last year of his life, Brigadier Robinson led the Garter procession down the hill, puffing and wheezing, a considerable distance for an old man. Such is the spirit of a Military Knight.

I spent a lot of time at St George's Chapel during my

school years. It was a great passion of mine. I had first visited Windsor Castle when I was eight, taken there by my parents on a Sunday outing in 1960. Easter fell early in 1964 and we had not yet gone home for the school holidays. We were taken from my prep school in Englefield Green to hear the St John Passion at St George's Chapel. I remember queuing for what seemed a very long time. Our headmaster kept us interested by telling us a little of the history of the Chapel. He talked of the royal vault, and the mysterious way the coffin would disappear into the ground during a royal funeral, leaving a precarious hole. I heard too of the Knights of the Garter, whose banners hung in the Quire.

Quite why I found it all so fascinating I cannot explain, but I resolved to discover it for myself when the opportunity presented itself. I did not have to wait long. In September that year, on my first Saturday at Eton I made my way up the hill and bought a ticket to St George's Chapel. I went back every available Saturday and Sunday thereafter for the next five years.

Sometimes I asked questions, learning the history of the Chapel. I began to work out which banner belonged to the Queen and where she sat. In due course I deciphered the banners of the other Knights of the Garter. I attended chapel services and ceremonies. I took it all very seriously. I recently discovered a school report which mentioned that on a particular Sunday evening in October 1967 I was wearing a mournful expression. I told my modern tutor that this was because Lord Attlee had died. When questioned further, I apparently revealed that my sadness did not stem from an admiration of Lord Attlee's policies, but because his death reduced the number of the Knights of the Garter!

During my school holidays I constructed a model of St George's Chapel which took up an entire room. I recreated all the detail including the heraldic banners, and gradually I peopled it with some five hundred little figures made by me and observed from life. It was thus that I became particularly familiar with the faces of the individual Military Knights of the day.

In February 1966 I became a chapel guide under a scheme instigated by the energetic Dean of Windsor, Robin Woods. We showed tourists round the Chapel on Sunday afternoons. After this we were invariably invited to tea by a Military Knight and his wife. Being a chapel guide did not automatic-ally lead to a meeting with Major Clough, however. As he was a widower, he did not offer the boys tea. Besides, he was very much older than his colleagues.

In 1967, about a year after his ninetieth birthday, Major Clough was obliged to lay aside his uniform and march no more. Old age overcame him and he retired to his bed, dying very slowly over a period of three years. We often asked about Major Clough. I rather think that it was Brigadier Robinson, with his cavalier attitude to such matters, who explained his non-appearance those days as 'Cloughy's waterworks giving him a spot of bother'.

One afternoon in 1969 I asked one of the Minor Canons how Major Clough was. He used to take him communion in his house, and, encouraging my unspoken wish to meet him, suggested that I should call on him one afternoon. He thought this would be a constructive diversion for the aged soldier. A while later, on 13 September, a meeting was arranged and I duly presented myself at number 7 Lower Ward.

Major Clough was bedridden, and he was being cared for by a very kind friend called Christian Kappey. She answered the door and took me into his drawing-room where the bed was made up. I soon learned that she spent all her time with him and would even sleep night after night on an uncomfortable Victorian sofa in this room. The Major had shrunk since I had last seen him out and about. His face was soft and pink and his hair thick and white. His eyes were set deep in somewhat bloodshot sockets. He was obviously in some discomfort, but he was lucid and enjoyed talking for a little while, and showing me his scrapbook, which was a curious mixture of military pictures and photographs of the Royal Family interspersed with naked and well-endowed young ladies prised from the inner pages of tabloid newspapers and elsewhere.

The first visit was memorable for a rather unpleasant incident which occurred just as I was leaving the house. A hearse from E. Sargeant & Son, Windsor's undertakers, was drawn up outside the garden of Henry VIII Gateway, and a body was being carried out on a stretcher. Covered only by a blanket, the shape of the corpse was clearly visible, the feet and the head. The body could have come from one of two houses, that of a Mr Kennedy or that of another Military Knight, Brigadier Furze, whom I had known for three years. I felt rather sick but had to wait until the following day to find out who it was. Selfishly, I was relieved when I saw the bespectacled Brigadier marching into chapel as usual. Prayers were then said for the deceased James Kennedy.

My first visit to Major Clough was considered a success and it soon became a regular Saturday occasion. Tea was the time for visitors, and as the weeks went by I met a number of other friends who would come in to cheer the Major up. One of these was Christian's sister, Joan, who was living in their house in Clarence Road, just beyond the roundabout on the Windsor relief road. Both sisters were cheerful and good-hearted people, smiling through difficult and sad lives. Christian was clearly devoted to Major Clough, and was doing her best to make his last days happy and comfortable. She often used to comment: 'Old age is so sad. It's such a crime!' She hated to see her splendid, upright old friend reduced to the bed-ridden state. Although Joan was the older of the two, she had none of the authority of an elder sister. She was friendly from the start and not long before I left school she invited me to lunch with her at Clarence Road. Christian hoped to be able to get away, but in the event she was unable to do so.

I was nearing the end of my schooldays and was allowed more freedom than in earlier times. I was able to get away for lunch on a Sunday in November. Schoolboys walked every-where, and I made my way to the house on foot. It was a considerably longer journey than I had anticipated. That was all right except that time was against me and I knew that I would have to leave early. It is a particular agony to be still at the table knowing that presently you have to make an excuse, jump up and leave before the coffee.

3

The Man in the Photograph

The house at which I arrived was a tall, upright Victorian semi-detached with a small overgrown garden at the front and a larger better-kept garden at the back. The sisters had lived there most of their lives, certainly ever since they returned to England from India. The exterior was forbidding and badly kept, with a small white gate with the name 'Dargai' hand-painted on it somewhat amateurishly. The interior of the house had scarcely changed during their occupancy. It was completely Edwardian and decorated as in their late mother's day.

Both sisters had their own territory within the house, which they guarded zealously. This meant that on the ground floor each had her own sitting-room. Joan, being the elder, had the room at the front. Joan's sitting-room had chintz sofas and chairs, all rather worn, small side tables, a mantelpiece covered with old invitations, Christmas cards and Garter programmes, and photographs of the family and her special friends. Her mother looked austere as seen in old age, with long white hair dressed like a child's. She was photographed slumbering in their garden in the last year of her life. There was a soldier in uniform with an older lady, this a beloved friend of both sisters, called Harry Jacob, with Violet Erskine Jacob, his mother. It transpired that he had been killed in the First World War, one of so many similar tragedies, while she was well known as an author in Scotland.

Likewise in a silver frame stood a young lady of fashion in fancy dress, photographed by Lafayette. This was Lady Dorothy Palmer, a niece of Lord Alfred Douglas (the friend of Oscar Wilde). Unlike many of the others in frames, she had survived into old age and was to be a fellow lunch guest that day. Then on the walls of the room were later additions, not very good paintings of horses, of the variety that can be bought ready-framed in Woolworths. On one wall behind the sofa was a large Edwardian portrait of a lady in evening dress wearing a foreign decoration. Disdainful of manner, haughty of appearance, she dominated the room. This was Joan's Aunt Clare, who liked to call herself la Comtesse Morel des Boullets. She had married a French Count, who was in reality a Turk attached to the delegation in London. His name was Morel Bey, and his portrait hung elsewhere in the house.

Other adornments of the room included postcards, photos, and calendars bearing the Queen's image. There was a corner cupboard containing fine china, and a quite handsome old chest covered with a rug. Joan was something of a do-it-yourself expert and had gilded some of her furniture. She had also gilded the surround to the overhead light.

That in essence was the ordinary decoration of the room. But there was that other feature which the first-time visitor could not fail to notice. On every wall, in every corner, framed identically, there was a hand-coloured image of a man. There were in fact two images. In the more striking of the two, he was seated in a chair, in tweed jacket and tie, photographed in the room in which his picture now stood. The other photograph had been taken in the garden, the same man on the same day, this time his trousers more of a feature hanging rather baggily about him. It was impossible to look anywhere without seeing this man. He glanced back at you from every angle. He looked a little surly, probably reluctant to be captured on film. It was impossible to escape his gaze.

Inevitably I wondered who the man was, and why his image was on every wall. But on this, my first visit, I was not bold enough to ask. Joan would talk about her mother, her brother (then living in South Africa), about Harry Jacob and Aunt Clare. But she did not allude to the man in the photograph.

Lady Dorothy Palmer arrived for lunch. She was old and infirm, bearing scant resemblance to her Lafayette photograph. She was also as good as stone deaf so it was virtually impossible to talk to her. My abiding memory of her is an agony of nervous silence, broken occasionally by her saying 'Yerss'. The isolation of her deafness must have been tiresome for her too. I have every reason to believe that she was a sweet-natured person. Joan was devoted to her and had her to lunch every Sunday. This was her only square meal of the week. Otherwise she subsisted on 'Meals on Wheels'. After every invitation Lady Dorothy would return to her cottage at Oakley Green and write a more or less identical letter of thanks: 'My dearest Joan, I did so enjoy my day with you last Sunday, thank you so very much . . .'

Apparently her late husband, Captain Esmond Palmer, had virtually drunk her out of the house. Lady Dorothy would return to find items of furniture sold to finance his unfortunate habit. Joan and Lady Dorothy shared a passion for cats, and were old friends who had said over the years all they were ever going to say to each other.

I recall the small glass of sherry before lunch, in the preparation of which Joan slaved in the kitchen. Then we went through to an ice-cold dining-room, part of the kitchen, with linoleum floor and a large painted wooden kitchen dresser. We ate one of those essentially English meals that are reminiscent of the worst kind of school lunch, tasteless meat, huge boiled potatoes and somewhat stewed brussels sprouts. It was the kind of meal that took hours to prepare and yet tasted awful. Being at school at the time, this seemed normal enough fare. As at school the lunch was preceded by grace, Joan closing her eyes and mouthing a silent prayer.

My overriding memory of that first lunch at Clarence Road is of having to rush away in order to get back to school in time. However, I must have acquitted myself well enough, for the invitation was repeated.

At the second lunch, on a rather overcast Friday in December, I found myself seated once more in Joan's sitting-room with the haunting image of the man staring at me from every corner. I still did not know who he was, and I still did not have the courage to ask Joan about him.

This time there were two other guests, both elderly ladies from grand Irish families. Neither of them paid the slightest attention to the photograph, which both took for granted. I had no idea whether or not either of them knew the man. As it was later to turn out, they were both closely involved with him.

The two ladies lived at The Links at Ascot, a house I was to hear a lot more about later. The larger of them was called Mrs Bonham. I did not find her particularly friendly. She was rather on the severe side. She wore dull grey and dark blue clothes, a beret on her white hair and no make-up.

Mrs Bonham was accompanied by another old lady called Frances Kavanagh, known to her friends as Francie. She was the owner of The Links, a spinster with a very attractive smile and a lyrical laugh. Though badly crippled with arthritis and very thin, her attitude to life was wholly positive. She had a sense of fun. She was the kind of old person who was a young person grown old. Time had changed her outward appearance but not her inner self. This was not true of Mrs Bonham.

She was an old person in the accepted sense, and I got the impression that she grumbled about everything.

Looking back as I do years later, it is hard to be sure exactly how much I knew then compared with what I found out later. Miss Kavanagh had an imposing family history, the details of which were revealed to me gradually over a period of time. Certainly the world of Anglo-Irish gentry enjoying life to the best of their ability despite infirmity and with limited financial resources was one I had not met before.

Miss Kavanagh was descended from the ancient Kings of Leinster. She too was linked to the Military Knights. Her father, Lieutenant-General Sir Charles McMorrough Kavanagh, had been Governor of the Military Knights from 1932 until his death in 1950, when General Hakewill Smith took over. She had therefore lived in the Mary Tudor Tower (sometimes known as the Governor's Tower) for a great number of years. Before that her father had served in the South African War, like Major Clough, and had commanded the mobile column in Cape Colony from 1901 to 1902. He later commanded the Cavalry Brigade. In the Castle he was affectionately known as 'Puffing Billy' because of his habit of drawing in a quantity of breath and emitting it in great huffs and puffs as he walked along.*

Miss Kavanagh had played polo in India as a girl. She told me that she was in the Mary Tudor Tower the night of the

* The General was the son of Rt. Hon. Arthur McMorrough Kavanagh, known as 'The McMorrough' (1831–1889). An Irish politician, he was a most remarkable character, who was born with only the rudiments of arms and legs and yet travelled in remote parts of Asia. He was a keen shot, angler and yachtsman, he rode to hounds, chopped down trees with his axe, and was a fair amateur draughtsman. In the library of the House of Commons he moved about by short springs on his stumps from one shelf to another, and never sought help.

Abdication. She recalled Lord Wigram coming in to see her father and declaring, 'It's the best news possible. The King is going.' That kind of story had great appeal for a future biographer, who did not yet know that this would be his career in life.

I continued to pay regular visits to Major Clough and Christian, and I always considered Christian to be my particular friend of the two sisters. I so admired her care of Major Clough, having never before or since witnessed such total dedication. Major Clough's father had been an Etonian, and he held my school in high esteem. When I left the College at the end of that year he presented me with an Old Etonian tie, which I rather think he expected me to wear every day from that day on.

Leaving school meant that I was not at Windsor so regularly. However, old diaries reveal that whenever possible I would go to tea at number 7 Lower Ward, or to lunch at Clarence Road. Gradually I became part of this curious group of friends, which was an extensive but close network.

The cornerstone of the group was the house at Ascot, known as The Links. I learned that Miss Kavanagh lived there with a man called Colonel Louis Murphy, a diminutive soldier who slightly reminded me of the kind of figure that Dick Emery, the comedian, would impersonate. He remains a rather mysterious figure. His real name was Michael Aloysius Murphy. There is even more than a little doubt as to whether or not he was a real Colonel. I was given the impression that the Colonel was Miss Kavanagh's boyfriend but that he and Miss Kavanagh had never married. I supposed this was because she had been kept at home for so long. Now, it seems that he was more of a general factotum at The Links, unlikely ever to have married. Nevertheless, whenever I saw Miss Kavanagh, 'Colonel' Murphy was with her.

Francie moved to The Links in about 1954, after her parents' death.* I first went to the house in the autumn of 1970. It proved to be the home of a great number of disparate characters, including, as it transpired, the man in the photograph.

One day there came an opportunity to ask Joan about the photograph. She was talking about her brother, Reggie, and I asked mock-innocently if he was the man in the picture. 'Oh no,' she replied, 'that's my Dick.' It transpired that he was called Dick Bonham, and was the son of the same Mrs Bonham who had lunched on my second visit. Joan said no more, but implied that he was a dearly loved friend. At some point the mystery deepened when I noticed that she wore a bracelet with her name and his and the date 1960. Had they had an affair? What did it all mean? Why was his photograph staring at us all the time? The picture was on such public display. His mother had sat in the room with her son staring back at her, yet passed no comment. Nor did any of the others. Clearly they all knew the circumstances, but I was not admitted to that secret. This was as it should have been, of course. Besides, from all I ever knew or later learned about the whole group, they were not mischief-makers.

There occurred an extraordinary development on 14 May 1970. I went down to Windsor to see Major Clough and Christian and to have lunch with them. This was a special treat, as tea was the normal hour of entertainment. I had been away so there was a lot to talk about. I returned to London in good humour. That very afternoon I went to have tea with Mrs Norma Sadleir, another Irish lady with a beaming smile, who lived in Queen's Gate. She was the widow of Ulster King-of-Arms and her grandson had been at school with me. While

* Her mother, Lady Kavanagh, suffered from arteriosclerosis and died in Holloway Sanatorium, following a fall downstairs, aged eighty-three.

we were talking the doorbell rang and she told me that the man who tended her window-boxes was arriving.

In walked the man in the photograph – Dick Bonham. Admittedly he was slightly older, but it was without doubt him. He still wore the same style of clothes, baggy trousers and a tweed jacket. He had put on weight. He looked rather like a prep school maths master. He was friendly but somewhat surprised when I felt obliged to admit: 'I know who you are. I have seen your photograph.' He quickly surprised me in return by saying, 'We have never met. You must never say you have seen me. It is a very difficult situation.' He implied that Joan had some kind of fixation about him, was always sending him Bemax and other unwanted gifts, that much of his life was spent trying to fend her off. He spoke of his life at The Links with Francie Kavanagh, Colonel Murphy and the others. He was a landscape gardener by profession and travelled about doing work for the network of friends. He seemed contented in his work and certainly Mrs Sadleir was devoted to him.

It was such a strange coincidence to meet him, especially as I had been in the Kappey world earlier in the day. I suppose it was odd to find him such a natural person, a normal everyday man. His photograph had made him appear rather sinister, and its multiplication hinted at a certain glamour that was not apparent that afternoon. It was intriguing to wonder what he had done to get himself transformed into an icon. He clearly meant so much to Joan Kappey. She worshipped him.

Meeting him in London was also rather odd. He did not belong there in my imagination. He belonged to the Kappey world, Windsor and Ascot, a world fixed in the shadow of the Castle. I wondered about so much and never thought I would know the answer to so many unasked questions. Twenty years would pass before I knew the ramifications of the story in full detail.

I left Mrs Sadleir's flat after tea. With the enthusiasm of youth, I longed to tell my story. I remember feeling disappointed that nobody found it remotely interesting at the time.

4

The Death of Major Clough

On his last birthday, just before Christmas 1969, Major Clough received thirty bottles of Moët et Chandon, five and a half bottles of whisky, seven plants, twenty-four cards, two telegrams and various other presents, which as Christian noted was 'not bad for ninety-three!' But his general state of health was poor and he suffered several bad haemorrhages, and later had much trouble with his glands.

In the summer of 1970 the heat made his life very uncomfortable. He was able to get into his wheelchair a couple of times and one afternoon he sat in his garden, but the effort made him very tired. In July Christian wrote me one of many letters from the Lower Ward describing his gradual sinking: 'I have had a very worrying time with poor old Billy, who is a *very* sick man – & it's *so* distressing to see his slow, & somewhat torturous decline – it almost makes one lose faith, to see the *old* being made to suffer – but he is so *brave* – & at times looks *very* well. Everyone says so.' Then in August the decline was worse:

I am having a very distressing time, as poor Billy's arm is much worse, it has opened, & has to be dressed twice a day by the District Nurses who are a power of strength, but it entails a lot of work for me. In other ways he is a lot weaker. I only hope that he will pass peacefully in his sleep when the time comes, & that he will not have to be rushed into

Hospital or a Home, so please say a prayer for the poor old darling.

The end came soon afterwards. Major Clough died at home in Christian's arms on 10 September, and I heard the news from her exactly a year to the day after our first meeting. I attended his funeral a week later in St George's Chapel. The funerals of Military Knights are always rather impressive, the plumed hat resting on the Union flag on top of the coffin, and the surviving Knights lining up to give the cortège a farewell salute. They take these events in their stride. I remember the widow of one of the Knights, setting off down the hill after another such funeral, commenting, 'Ah well, that's another one gone. It's always sad when one goes!' Christian wrote later: 'It was a very nice service, *except* for the really terrible *faux pas* the General [Sir Edmund Hakewill Smith] made in not arranging for a Bugler to sound the Last Post & Reveille, & a dead march. To me the whole thing was spoilt. Billy was so *essentially* a soldier & it was his last right. However, it all went off well otherwise.'

Christian accompanied the coffin on the long car journey to Nottinghamshire, to his childhood home in Clifton-cum-Glapton (as it is now known). That riparian parish, once set so securely in the countryside, was now an isolated rustic enclave, hemmed in by a network of orange-lit ring roads and the spreading industrialization of Long Eaton and Nottingham. There Major Clough was buried in a grave beside his wife, in the shadow of the church. Christian wrote a note in her diary: 'I followed him to his last rest – with my heart breaking.'

5

The Inmates of The Links

It was only a few days after Major Clough's funeral that I accepted a longstanding invitation from Miss Kavanagh to lunch at The Links. I took what seemed an expensive taxi from Windsor to Ascot (it cost me a pound) and arrived at the other establishment that is important in this story. I was keenly interested to see it. This was where the man in the photograph lived. And it was my opportunity to get to know the inmates of the house.

The Links was a large house which rather resembled one of those Surrey preparatory schools. I remember where it was, but now the house has gone. It must have been pulled down in recent years and replaced with a series of new, smaller houses.

Opposite Ascot racecourse, on the Windsor Road, The Links was set in a gravel drive, bordered with rhododendron. The house was spacious inside, with a large, heavily gilded drawing-room overlooking the lawn, and a good-sized dining-room. In winter the drawing-room was brighter than in the summer, when the windows were rather closely overhung with foliage. But there was nothing claustrophobic about it. Here Miss Kavanagh presided over her group of old folk, whose foibles were accepted and tolerated in a most commendable way.

The Links was Miss Kavanagh's home. She ran it as a community, a kind of self-supporting old folk's home, where the inmates contributed something towards their upkeep. Some of them lived there all the time, others (like Dick Bonham's mother) came and went (she spent part of the year in Ireland). There was no shortage of drama with so many disparate types gathered under one roof. Occasionally one of the residents proved unsatisfactory. There had been a businessman, whom none of the others knew. He rented a room for a time. He was asked to leave when a woman was found in his room.

The inmates had great bridge tournaments in the evenings and big parties at seasons such as Christmas and New Year. Joan often wrote to me of the fun they had: 'Everywhere looked most festive, with a lovely Christmas tree and huge log fire burning in the drawing-room, & liqueurs after coffee. All very luxurious.'

The highlight of their year was Royal Ascot week, during which they threw open the large garden and at five pounds a car allowed car-parking for four days running. Christian once wrote to me that they parked 138 cars in a day. They worked hard, and somehow coped with the damage to the lawn if Ascot was wet. They were then given a splendid tea with strawberries and cream. At the end of the week the takings were totted up (perhaps as much as two thousand pounds). There was an additional incentive for the car-parkers: their reward. A few weeks later a bus was hired and twenty-two of them went up to London to see some popular theatre or film and to dine afterwards at the old Caprice (no doubt reminding many of their younger days). They returned to Ascot somewhat blotto, having blown a great deal of the money. One year Miss Kavanagh was taken to court, rather unsportingly, by the Income Tax people for not declaring her Ascot takings.

The inmates got the most out of life. None had much money, many had awful aches and pains, but their spirits were good. Once they went on an expedition to Longleat. While the ladies waited patiently outside, Miss Kavanagh's friend, Colonel Murphy, insisted on leading the men through Lord Weymouth's private suite of muralled rooms, which included the celebrated Kama Sutra bedroom. The old boys came out into the fresh air somewhat bedazzled.

Lunching at The Links was a memorable experience. Although the food was again of the stewed brussels sprouts variety and there was only water at the table, your particular host looked after you in the drawing-room before lunch. You were conducted to an alcove overlooking the garden, where there were a number of bottles, each one belonging to one or other of the inmates. You were encouraged to help yourself liberally to spirits to perk you up before lunch. The levels of the bottles may well have been marked.

On the day I lunched at The Links a number of the old folk were present. Amongst them was Dick Bonham. While Miss Kavanagh presided, the next in the pecking order was Colonel Murphy. He was the man who reminded me of Dick Emery, and he scampered about in brightly coloured clothes, his hair brushed over his forehead in a fringe, a cravat round his neck and his pipe in his hand. His particular responsibility at The Links was the garden. Upstairs he had decorated his room with exotic Chinese fabrics and artifacts. He took me up there and showed it to me and I must confess I had never seen anything similar. He was clearly very proud of it. It was curious to find such a room recreated so close to Ascot racecourse.

An eventful military career had led the Colonel to The Links. He was born in 1890. As a young man he served in the First World War in Mesopotamia and then the Iraq operations of 1919–20. In the early 1920s he was employed with the Egyptian Army and from 1925 to 1931 he was attached to the Sudan Defence Force. The year 1935 found him as officer in charge of regimental records at Woolwich. Though some at The Links thought he was a Lieutenant-Colonel, Irish Guards, he was in reality a Major in the Royal Army Veterinary Corps. Just before the Second World War he was attached to the British troops in China as Deputy Assistant Director of Veterinary Services.

Miss Kavanagh had to make excuses for the next inmate, and Miss Kavanagh was very good at expressing the line that was to be taken about certain things. Lady Mant would be at lunch, though she was not in the drawing-room before it. She was the widow of Sir Reginald Mant, KCSI, KCIE, a member of the Indian Civil Service and one-time Member of the Council of India. Lady Mant was herself the daughter of a Colonel in the Indian Medical Service. Miss Kavanagh warned me with a simple smile that Lady Mant would not speak to me at all during lunch. This I was not to mind. She had not spoken for some years now, and she was a hundred.* I felt sure she would say something, but I was completely wrong. She sat opposite me, looking at each speaker in turn with gimlet eyes, and diligently ate a square meal with the help of a small Anglepoise lamp which lit her plate. When she had finished eating, she folded the lamp neatly, got up from the table and set off for a long walk around Ascot. She never spoke and I never saw her again.

Another resident at The Links was a man called 'Tod' Body, a retired chartered surveyor, whose nephew is the Eurorebel Tory MP Sir Richard Body. Tod was of the party that memorable day. He spoke in such a falsetto voice that, with the cruelty of youth, I found myself wondering if he had been castrated. He was a friendly character, taking life in his stride.

* I later discovered, to my disappointment, that in fact she was only ninety-five.

Not present that day, but much in evidence later, was a rather dubious bachelor historian called Jim Lonsdale Bryans. He had been through Eton and Balliol and was descended from a Bishop. His health had declined after the First World War, following which he had surrendered what he considered a promising diplomatic career and passed his time circumnavigating the globe, 'combined with a close, and at moments intimate, observation of international affairs'. He was proud to describe himself as an amateur, explaining, 'The amateur presumably, not to say etymologically, is he who does for the love of the thing what the professional does for mixed motives.' Lonsdale Bryans was often to be found poised over a sketchbook, 'always an excellent means of cultivating chance acquaintances'.

Lonsdale Bryans wrote and published an apologia for his bizarre efforts in the Second World War. The gist of *Blind Victory* was that had the Foreign Office trusted him to pursue his ideas, Hitler would have been overthrown and an honourable peace achieved between Britain and Germany. In this somewhat gripping book, he described himself as 'Mr X. of the von Hassell Diaries', explaining that he forged secret links with Ulrich von Hassell* and sought to assure him of the backing of the British government in his endeavours to overthrow Hitler.

In the midst of his campaign he found himself on alien soil. Though a Balliol man, he resorted to techniques more akin to a spy thriller. His efforts included what he clearly took to be a convincing impersonation of American vernacular. He sent a telegram: 'Gee but I was darn glad to get your wire and letter . . .' Unfortunately the British government took a

---

* Baron Ulrich von Hassell (1881–1944), former German Ambassador in Rome. He was executed for his part in the plot of 20 July 1944.

dim view of Lonsdale Bryans fraternizing with German nationals, in English or American, and the Permanent Under-Secretary at the Foreign Office, Sir Alexander Cadogan, recorded his lack of charm and how he could not wait to get him out of the room.†

Old Jim was a painter, not a very good one, favouring bird and animal pictures and religious ceremonies on tropical islands. (I remember seeing one of his daubs of Princess Anne amidst the dreadful wedding presents on show at St James's Palace in 1973. He had sent it to her, unsolicited.) He worked at night, and liked to muse: 'Midnight is the noon of thought.'

Lonsdale Bryans was a talkative old boy, possibly rather intense. His travels had taken him to Spain during the Revolution and to the Tropics. He also composed music. He had a book of memoirs in the offing, *The Green Flash*.* This was never published. He puffed away at an old pipe and looked as though he needed someone to take care of him. At The Links, he was the inmate the others loved to hate. The older he became, the more his table manners deteriorated. Egg stains adorned his Old Etonian tie. Eventually he was banned from the dining-room altogether. Thereafter he dined from a tray in his room.

Lunch was served in the dining-room, everyone seated at a large table and served by a grim-looking maid. With the notable exception of Lady Mant, the inmates were talkative and friendly. Miss Kavanagh sat at the head of the table, and though a quiet person, could always command the attention

† Nevertheless the file relating to Lonsdale Bryans's dealings with von Hassell is still sealed at the Public Record Office.

* Lonsdale Bryans called it *The Green Flash* in tribute to the phenomenon that occurs at sunset. The last light before the red glow fades is a flash of green lasting less than a quarter of a second. Only a quarter of the population can see it. He had been one of the fortunate ones.

of the room when she spoke. Traditional views were expressed about the iniquities of the government, the latest royal story was relayed in tones of respect, the cost of living was politely decried. There was also much laughter and fun at the table, and even I as a youngster was given a good hearing.

Dick Bonham loved talking about his Irish ancestry. He was fascinated by it in a way that is only possible in one who has done nothing to further his own line. He loved to talk of Hamilton and Bonham cousins, of whom there appeared to be a considerable number. The one subject he never referred to again was the obsession that Joan had for him.

I understood that I was not to mention to Joan that I had seen Dick on any specific occasion. Even Christian refrained from mentioning that she was going to The Links if Dick was there. Gradually, however, it was accepted that we had met. That Christmas Joan referred to him in a letter to me: 'We have had several very nice New Year Luncheons & Dinners, the *nicest* for *me*! was with dearest Dick Bonham, & his dear mother at "The Links" with dear Frances Kavanagh & Louis.' I do remember being alarmed once when Joan said something about Dick that was clearly untrue. I happened to know that he was away, yet she said, 'I was talking to my dear friend Dick about that only last night.' It could not have happened and it worried me. I was young and adults surely did not tell lies, especially not pointless ones. It was a fantasy lie.

In a way it was curious to find Dick Bonham living at The Links. He was a good twenty years younger than the others, yet he was an integral part of the team. He was there because his mother lived there. He was clearly the mainstay of the place, doing a great number of chores and helping Miss Kavanagh in innumerable ways. He and his car were always available to give a lift if need be and, being a gardener, he helped Colonel Murphy with the extensive garden. Unlike the others, he was away a lot, working elsewhere, but he obviously felt totally at ease in his surroundings. Evelyn Waugh would have described him as 'a jagger'.

I was still fascinated that the man in the photograph had come to life. He chatted away at the table, with spirited responses from Miss Kavanagh, the Colonel and Tod Body, and silence from Lady Mant.

Not long afterwards I went off to Strasbourg University for a year with kind messages from the two sisters. Christian wrote, 'Don't let the *wicked* world spoil you,' and Joan urged, 'Take care of your dear self, as there are some queer folk in the world, Hugo.' I did not doubt it but could not help wondering if any of them would be as strange as the inmates of The Links.

6

The Kappeys

I still knew very little about the Kappey sisters, but I know a
great deal more now. I came to know them better in the 1970s,
as I grew older. During those years I saw them often, usually at
Dargai, but occasionally at The Links. Christian used to take
me over there. I don't remember ever seeing Joan there. I also
used to meet Christian in London on her antiquing forays to
the capital and we would have coffee together at Fortnum's.

Gradually, I saw less of the sisters, and after Christian's
death I only saw Joan very occasionally. It was therefore a
considerable surprise to discover that just before she died,
Joan had appointed me as one of her two executors, presumably because I was a friend from a younger group, who had
nevertheless known her for more than a decade.

I saw Joan for the last time very shortly before her death in
November 1987 and I attended her funeral in Windsor, returning to her sitting-room for tea and biscuits with those of her
friends who had gathered for that last time. Soon afterwards I
returned there to help in the long business of tidying up the
house and preparing it for sale on behalf of the estate. It was a
strange experience to return to the house where I had paid my
first shy visit almost twenty years before. This time the house
was empty save for my co-executor going about his business
elsewhere on the premises.

Joan's front room was where she had spent her days and

nights in the last months of her life. Opposite its door was the entrance to Christian's sitting-room, unused since her death. The stairs were between the two. I had been upstairs before, because the bathroom was on the first floor. It was rather a bleak room and on a winter's day one did not linger there. It was painted a somewhat institutional green and there were many damp patches and exposed pipes. I am glad I never had to have a bath in it.

The main bedroom on the first floor was above Joan's sitting-room. This was old Mrs Kappey's room and it was still furnished as in her day. Her dressing-table and many of her personal effects were still there, although I later discovered that she had died as long ago as 1961. I am not clear whether this room was used or not or whether it had been left as a kind of shrine. I suspect the latter. In the room were many bundles of old letters, kept as they always had been. These included family papers and diaries, letters from their father, Major Kappey, in India and photographs of life in India at the time of the Raj. There were invitations from maharajahs, concert programmes, tickets, and other indications of a carefree life long passed in happier times.

Joan's bedroom was opposite, next to the bathroom and overlooking the garden at the back of the house. Here I found yet more versions of the photograph of Dick Bonham, lined up on the dressing-table, and a quantity of calendars with dates ringed significantly. These indicated meetings with Dick or sightings of him. In a drawer there were bundles of writings in Joan's distinctive hand. These were drafts of letters that she had written to Dick over the years. There were other bundles of love-letters, neatly tied up in ribbons, mostly in chronological order. These pre-dated Dick and were post-marked in the 1930s or earlier.

Sorting the papers was a fairly dirty business because the

last years had been a time of such considerable decline. The house was cold and damp and parts of it were in a dismal condition. There was an additional hazard that alarmed me. The house had lately contained not only its lonely, almost blind owner, but a great number of cats. Some of these had been taken into care, but I was told that two particularly wild cats that had not been seen for some time had eluded detection and were still lurking somewhere in that derelict and now deserted domain. Every time I opened a cupboard I expected a ferocious cat to fly out at me, but as it happened they remained undisturbed in their hiding places.

I continued to wander about the upper rooms of the house with mixed emotions. On the one hand, I felt an intruder; on the other, I was increasingly fascinated by the lost world that lay undisturbed around me. I climbed to the top floor, where there were half a dozen books on the shelf. One of them was an anonymous book of memoirs written by Aunt Clare, the haughty lady in the portrait downstairs. I found photographs of her and of her Turkish husband, and a small red velvet box with an imperial cypher on it. The decoration that it had once contained had been removed by an unseen hand.

Christian had lived on the top floor in the 1970s and no doubt earlier. When the family first came to the house, this was where the nursery had been. Lately Christian had slept in one of these two rooms and had painted in the other. As she had predeceased Joan by some years, a certain amount of sorting had taken place up here. There was evidence of the careless removal of certain items of silver, often only the top layer of a box, the box itself remaining. Some of Christian's paintings were still there, an oil of Major Clough and other images of him. There was a portrait of her mother, executed by her from a photograph, and there was a trunk of clothes. These had come back from India with Mrs Kappey, and were

surprising because the waist of her dresses was almost imposs-
ibly slender.

One of my duties was to help arrange the sale of certain
items on behalf of the estate. The papers were destined for
the bonfire, but I expressed interest in them and was allowed
to take them away for sorting and reading, and in due course,
to find suitable homes for some of them. I went up and down
the stairs many times during this time and in the end more or
less filled my car with papers. They looked like junk when they
were all piled up and they smelt of cats. They must have
appeared very odd to a casual passer-by, but I think I already
knew that within these papers I would find missing clues to a
story, of which I knew only a fraction and which I had seen as
an observer so many years before.

Only a few of Christian's papers were still in the house, but
Mrs Kappey's were fairly complete and so were Joan's. The
Kappeys had never thrown anything away. There were news-
paper cuttings, family photographs, diaries and letters. There
were also a great number of palm crosses and other little
trinkets, all of which held significance of some kind. The
earliest letter I found was dated 1884.

In due course the sorting was done, the house was closed
down and it was sold. In the months that followed I occasionally drove past Clarence Road and noticed that the new
owner was restoring it, no doubt making it safe and comfortable and installing the many essentials that had been lacking
during the lives of the two sisters.

Back at home I set about sorting the papers. I was able to
piece together the story of the early lives of the Kappeys and
come to an understanding of how they reached the state in
which I found them in 1969. I read Aunt Clare's extraordinary
book of memoirs, which brought her vividly to life. And then
there was Dick Bonham. The papers unravelled something of

the mystery that surrounded the obsession that Joan suffered for Dick.

The obsession was the key to my interest. It dominated the lives of the Kappeys from 1960 onwards. But what of the long years that preceded it? What of the other icons in that old sitting-room in Clarence Road? These pictures could now be matched to the letters, and long-forgotten characters began to come to life again. I found I was just as interested in the Kappey parents. I found out where the Kappeys came from, what they might once have had, how they came to be living in the house in Windsor. I learned of the lives of their uncles and aunts, of their brother Reggie. I could trace their father's military service in India in the days of the Raj.

Although this is in many ways a sad story, it has elements of unsung courage and considerable generosity where resources were virtually non-existent. Inevitably I became fascinated by the whole group. It was impossible not to become intrigued by the plight of Lady Dorothy Palmer, the adventures of Aunt Clare and her Turk, the short service career of the ill-fated Harry Jacob.

I now had the skills of the biographer that I had lacked when I first went to the house in 1969. Given a clue, I knew how to follow it up and unravel the mysteries. I began my extensive research. There proved to be many clues for me to follow and I was soon engaged in an extensive quest, perusing old wills at Somerset House, travelling to the South Coast to inspect the wonderful reports that can be found in local newspapers of the period, and later still, I paid two visits to Ireland to find out more about Dick Bonham himself.

The saga began in the middle of the last century.

The Bandmaster

The Kappeys were a family of three, Reggie born in June 1897, Joan in July 1901, and Christian in January 1903. Their father was a soldier, Major Max Kappey, and their mother, Lily Mills, came from a large family of Millses, whose origins were in East Sussex.

The Kappeys came from Germany and before that from Hungary. There was a family of Kapy v. Kapivar recorded in the days of King Sigismund of Hungary (later German King and Roman Emperor). In the sixteenth century there were Kappes to be found in Württemberg. The grandfather, Jacob Adam Kappey (1825–1907), was a native of Hessen-Darmstadt, who left his homeland for political reasons following the German Revolution of 1848. He came to England, accompanied by his 'intimate friend and fellow thinker', the German poet Ferdinand Freiligrath (1810–1876), who wrote some of Germany's finest revolutionary songs, the first of which was *Ein Glaubensbekentniss* (1844). Freiligrath lived in exile in London until 1866, translating Burns, Longfellow, Tennyson and Shakespeare into German. He went back after the Amnesty, but Jacob Kappey stayed on.

Though his foremost interest was in politics, Kappey turned to a musical career as composer, editor and conductor of military music. He became Director of Music of the Royal Marines, Chatham division, editor of Boosey's *Military Journals*, and an examiner at Kneller Hall School of Music and the Royal Academy of Music. He also conducted the Rochester Choral Society, where his own cantata *Per Mare, Per Terram* was enthusiastically received. A comic opera that he wrote called *The Wager* was performed at the Gaiety Theatre in London and, at the time of his death, his *History of Military*

Music was the standard work on the subject. In the course of a long career he judged great brass band concerts in the North of England, and when he presented his collection of national songs to the British Museum, his gift was deemed 'a very valuable addition to our musical library'.

A Freemason, a Knight of Malta and a Knight of St John, he was remembered as a learned man, who retired into private life in 1891 and whose study 'became the well-loved centre of many literary, artistic and scientific friends, all of whom refer with affectionate regret and appreciation to the many happy hours they spent together there'. The naval architect Sir Philip Watts was one of his friends.

Jacob Kappey was a neat, balding figure, with white hair, a monocle, and a drooping moustache. In 1853 he married a lady christened Marie Appollonia, a stout, dull-looking Victorian, and they had three sons and three daughters, all rather different, it seems. When he died in December 1907 he left £980. His widow lived on at Chatham, a sufferer from chronic rheumatic arthritis for many years, dying aged eighty-seven in December 1916. One of the daughters, Sophie, known as Soph in the family, used to write stories and succeeded in getting some of them published. She was born in 1865, and was often in poor health. In May 1892 she married Alfred Hart, RN, and died aged thirty-two in 1898. A fortnight earlier, another daughter, Stella, had married a Belgian merchant called Albert Engelke, and lived mainly in Europe. Clare, the eldest, played a prominent part in the lives of her nieces. And then there were three brothers, Frederick and Ferdinand (known as Fred and Ferd) and Max.

Uncle Fred's Chinese Banner

Lieutenant-Colonel Frederick Kappey (1861–1919), a fierce, gruff-looking character, commanded the Royal Marine Artillery in China and received the medal for the Chinese operations from King Edward VII in person at Devonport in 1901. He joined the Marines in 1878 and saw action in the Egyptian Expedition of 1882. He enjoyed a varied military career, acquiring in China a red silk Chinese banner, of which he was very proud. He was given a gold and ivory paper-knife by the French Republic, and the Czar of Russia presented him with a 'most costly and massive' silver jewelled cigarette case to thank him for commanding the guard of honour on his arrival at Portsmouth. In September 1892 he married Mary Bayly, daughter of General Abingdon Augustus Bayly, Colonel Commandant of the Royal Artillery at Camberley. They had a son and daughter. It would seem that his marriage went wrong* as he left nothing to his wife or son, while he bequeathed a hundred pounds to a certain 'friend', Frances Palmer. He was at times 'fearfully pessimistic about his future outlook' (in his father's words).

During the Great War the Colonel served as Recruiting Staff Officer for the Royal Navy and Royal Marines, based at Southampton. He retired in April 1919 and shortly afterwards he came to an untimely end. One day in August he went bathing at Milford-on-Sea, suffered a heart attack in the sea and died. We know no more about him since he left instructions that his letters and diaries were to be destroyed unread.

---

* General Bayly, who died at Interlaken in 1900, made no mention of Mary or his Kappey grandchildren in his will.

Uncle Ferd's Odes

The other brother, Ferdinand (1866–1955), was variously described as a commercial agent, a retired literary critic and a rubber agent. As a young man he was lucky to be advanced £100 by his sister Stella's husband to set him up in business. He was something of a mystery to his parents as he went his own way, seemingly with success, but certainly without telling them anything about it. He published various volumes of poetry which might not perhaps find favour with a publisher today:

> As fades the breath upon a window-pane,
> As dies the colour from an evening sky,
> The fluctuant waves of our emotion die
> In seas of unremitting stress and strain . . .

Simpkin, Marshall, Hamilton, Kent & Co. published a volume of his *Sonnets and Lyrics* in 1899, and he received a more than enthusiastic review from George S. Hitchcock in the *Chatham Observer*, who went so far as to say:

By the favour of Divine Thought and by the grace of Poetry, Ferdinand Kappey is heir-apparent to the position of Rossetti. There are poems of his which have not one thought in common with Rossetti's, not a phrase nor a rhyme; and yet it might have been supposed they were written by the author of THE HOUSE OF LIFE, had they not been found in this volume. The type of mind is that of the Painter-poet, and succeeds as his in producing work that adds the power of thought to the charm of Edgar Allan Poe's and Baudelaire's rare and magical verse.

Ferdinand was also praised for some success with 'the

almost untranslatable poetry' of Heine. Soon afterwards his book was one of ten reviewed in *Speaker* by the depressive poet, John Davidson (the author of *Fleet Street Eclogues* – he swam out to sea off Penzance and drowned himself in a fit of depression in 1909). Davidson was dismissive about the other nine volumes, but concluded: 'But I have good wine to end with. Sweetness, grace, and strain of actual melancholy go to the making of Mr Kappey's sonnets and lyrics.' Ferd was also a good draughtsman, with a sense of humour when it came to a caricature. And he had a facility for versified humour:

> Ye devotees of Art – behold
> This study from the Nude!
> They're not from life – for *that*, I'm told,
> Is very very rude.

The poem's illustration was a pair of wooden artists' dummies. His fondness for poetry and drawing was inherited by Christian, his favourite niece. In 1888 he married Edith Hilliard, the daughter of a shipwright in Chatham, and produced a son (a civil servant), and two daughters, one of whom married a man called Percy Mott, evidently well known in Bohemian circles, who sang well and at one time backed theatrical shows with fair success. Ferd was widowed in 1940 and spent his last years in a flat in Ryde, in the Isle of Wight, and died at the age of eighty-eight. He left just under £7,000.

7

The Turkish Delights of Aunt Clare

Of all Joan and Christian's uncles and aunts it was Clare who was to exert the most influence. She lived until 1944 and it was her striking portrait in lavish evening dress that dominated the front drawing-room of 159 Clarence Road. Clare was born in 1860, and when she was twenty-five she married Morel Bey, Councillor at the Turkish Embassy in London from 1886 to 1896. It is my theory that Aunt Clare lived a life of myth, that she was not truthful, and that she was a troublemaker. In 1920 she wrote an anonymous book of memoirs called *From an Eastern Embassy*, which was published by Herbert Jenkins. Evidently she had been writing for the *Ladies' Field* under the pseudonym of 'Cecil Mar'. She also translated the memoirs of a legendary *femme fatale*, Helene von Donniges (Princess Racowitza), a racy document but nevertheless a fascinating one, replete with such phrases as: 'My father's family . . . were direct descendants of the Vikings, and the fiercest blood of the wild Norsemen ran in their veins.' Clare's translation, if coloured, was still a thoroughly competent document.

Well educated and multilingual, Clare seemed to possess an idiosyncratic style of writing, now somewhat dated. In common with a great number of such books, her memoirs relate various bizarre experiences with the occult, and drop a great number of names amongst the lengthy descriptions of travel overseas. There are occasional funny stories such as the

The man in the photograph

The opening of St George's House, October 1966. The Queen
with the Dean of Windsor, Major Clough in the background. Nearest
the Queen, Brigadier Robinson

Major Clough
outside his house

The inmates of The Links. *Seated:* Colonel Murphy and Miss Kavanagh. *Standing:* Christian, unknown and Dick Bonham

Old age. Christian nursing Major Clough

Icons at Clarence Road. (*Above left*) Lady Dorothy Palmer,
(*above right*) Major Max Kappey, (*below left*) Harry Jacob and his mother,
Violet, (*below right*) Reggie in the King's Own Scottish Borderers

Aunt Clare

Lucien Morel Bey

The Turk – Morel Bey

The Kappey family: Mr and Mrs Jacob Kappey, Clare, Max, Stella, Sophie, Ferdinand and Frederick

Max and Lily Kappey on their wedding day, 1895

Lily Kappey in India

Joan and Christian

Joan and Christian in India

Joan and Christian in India

incident when Rustem Pasha, the Turkish Ambassador, was passed a loving-cup. He glanced apprehensively at it because 'a friend had informed him that the *ratelier** of an aged official had once dropped into the huge silver goblet, causing consternation to both guests and servants who happened to be near him'.

Quite early in her book, Aunt Clare goes to some lengths to explain that her husband was a Frenchman, not a Turk, presumably because it was about the lowest thing you could do to marry a Turk in those days. In private life she called him 'Gaston', and when in France used what she called 'my French title' of Comtesse Morel des Boullets:

> My husband's French nationality was apparent at a glance, in spite of the red fez he always wore in common with all Turkish officials. He was a member of the old French nobility, of the family of the Comtes de Sauville and of Baron Rey, one of Napoleon's generals who figures in one of the battle pictures at Versailles. Born in Paris, where he was educated, he later on went to America. At the time of which I write he had collaborated with the Ambassador for over thirty years, and had become his right hand.

Clare went on to point out that the Ambassador, Rustem Pasha, was really an Italian, called Count de Marini. I have had a good look at several photographs and a handsome portrait of Clare's husband, Morel Bey, and regrettably his 'French nationality' is not at all apparent to me. His dark eyes, thick black beard and pointed ears and chin indicate to the viewer a Turk in all meanings of the word. Clare was exceedingly class-conscious, and, to be fair, must have found herself a bit lost amongst all those bearded, fez-topped men. Nobody

* The *ratelier* was the upper row of false teeth.

47

talked at mealtimes at the Embassy as the Pasha insisted that he should always speak first. He veered towards the silent, indicating that he wished more wine simply by tapping the glass. Clare wrote: 'Although in my native land, I often imagined myself to be in some Far Eastern city. Racial instincts and prejudices, dating from the nursery, although unvoiced, seemed ever-present when all the members of that cosmopolitan Embassy were gathered together.'

In those days Turkey was ruled by a Sultan, at that time Abdul Hamid II, to all intents and purposes the last Sultan of Turkey, who was proclaimed on 31 August 1876. His nickname was 'Bedros' or 'Kanli', which translates as 'Bloody'. Born in the Topkapi Palace in 1842, he succeeded his half-brother, Murad V, who was deposed by the Viziers on the grounds of incurable insanity (in fact his mind was enfeebled by drink). While Murad V languished in the Ciragan Sarayi until dying of diabetes, Abdul Hamid ruled as an absolute monarch. Most historians have described him as 'a fiend incarnate'; Gladstone called him 'the Great Assassin'.

In Abdul Hamid's day, the granting of decorations had become, in the words of Sir Edwin Pears (self-appointed historian of Constantinople), 'so common that any value they may ever have possessed had ceased to exist in the minds of respectable people'.* Thus the portrait of Clare's husband bedecked in stars and ribbons is not as impressive as it might perhaps appear.

Being attached to the Embassy, Aunt Clare was expected to accompany her husband and the Ambassador to Drawing-Rooms, State Balls and concerts, where, despite the Ambassador's pride, the Turkish delegation was treated with a certain amount of condescension as part of '*la diplomatie*

* *Forty Years in Constantinople*, 1916, p. 143.

sauvage et des pays chauds'. Queen Victoria used to receive for an hour, standing in front of an armchair in the centre of the dais, bestowing a 'benevolent, motherly smile at the nervousness of débutantes, who were privileged to kiss her hand'. Once at a State Ball, a friend pointed out to Morel Bey that his wife had danced several animated dances with a British officer. Morel Bey assured him this was her brother Fred, but, mused Clare, 'even State Balls are not above the breath of scandal.'

Clare was amused by the variety of foreign potentates who arrived in London for the Queen's Golden Jubilee in 1887, notably 'Her Royal Blackness, Queen Kapiolani, of the Sandwich Islands' (as Clare described her). She reported:

> We were at a reception given in the dusky Queen's honour at the Hawaiian Legation in Hyde Park Gate . . . The Queen sat on a dais *en grand decolleté* blazing with jewels, and took herself quite seriously in the role of reigning Sovereign . . . The Hawaiian national hymn, a curious minor chant, was played during the ceremony. The expression on the faces of the ladies behind Her Majesty was a sight not easily to be forgotten!

Much of the time Clare was kept busy with official receptions, taking dictation from Morel Bey, or translating Gladstone's speeches and other documents into French. She also deciphered telegrams with the help of the Ambassador's code book. For this she was awarded a Turkish decoration for ladies, the Chefakat, or Order of Mercy (which she wears in her portrait). Ignoring Sir Edwin Pears's pronouncements on the subject, she mentions the honour with pride in her book. In her moments of spare time Clare dabbled in the occult, attended seances and indulged in the practice of chiromancy. She enjoyed talking to the Italian Ambassadress, Countess Tornielli, about the cultivation of happiness, 'not easy to find within ourselves, and impossible to find elsewhere'.

Clare's 'beloved son, only child and dearest friend', Lucien, known as 'Bunchy' in the family, was born on 15 April 1888. Rustem Pasha was his godfather and used to like to sit next to the golden-locked child. Later, while the Ambassador, then seventy-six, fell asleep over a dispatch at his desk, Clare would read to her son in the Embassy's centre room. As Rustem Pasha's health declined and he could eat nothing except oysters and turtle soup, Clare spent many weeks lunching alone with him. He died at last on 20 November 1895 and was buried at St Mary's, Kensal Green. Morel Bey did not wish to serve the new Ambassador; thus he and Clare, and young Lucien, set off 'to the land that was to play such a sinister role in modern times'. Morel Bey was appointed Chargé d'Affaires in the Turkish Embassy in Berlin, arriving there in the hot summer of 1896.

Berlin afforded the Morel Beys their first chance to lead a life of their own. Young Lucien was sent to be educated at the French Gymnasium, an institution founded by the Huguenots. Even so, the parents had to be vigilant and undo the patriotic indoctrination of national songs: 'All I have and all I am, I owe to thee my Fatherland'. Clare's memoirs are written as if she were wholly English. There is no mention of her own German ancestry, nor of her father's political commitments.

Clare's predilection for reading palms and clairvoyance led her into the realm of trouble: 'My fortune-telling proclivities were soon bruited abroad, and my life was made a perfect burden to me.' Otherwise her life was again a round of court balls and gala operas, this time presided over by the Kaiser. Their summer holidays were spent either at a seaside resort on the Baltic, or in the Black Forest. Clare wrote of Berlin:

As time went on we noticed a great difference in everything in Berlin. The arrogance of the military set grew rapidly, and civilians, old and young, rich and poor, became of secondary importance. Ladies often had to get off the pavement to make room for the swaggering wearer of a uniform . . .

Night-life in Berlin was truly remarkable. I often wondered when the people slept. The cafés in the Friedrichstrasse, Unter den Linden, and other streets, were ablaze with light until the morning hours were well advanced. Bread-winners and raw youths wandered from one café to another until long past dawn, although the strenuous day's work began at seven or eight in the morning.

It was in Berlin that Clare made friends with Princess Racowitza, of whom she wrote:

> Her life was full of love episodes, for she was a most beautiful woman and full of sentiment. Hers were not merely straw fires of emotion, but romances. As I sat on the balcony overlooking her little garden, years rolled back as Time's sweet-scented manuscript was unfolded in the shrine of her memory, and I listened to pages of a human document inscribed in indelible characters on a woman's stormy heart.

Evidently Ferdinand Lassalle, the German socialist who had been imprisoned for a year after the 1848 Revolution, fell madly in love with her and fought a duel with Prince Racowitza on her behalf in 1864. Lassalle died of a mortal wound and the incident formed the basis for George Meredith's novel, *The Tragic Comedians*. Petted by Hans Christian Andersen as a child, and the playmate of the young Ludwig of Bavaria, Helene later married Racowitza, but was soon widowed when he died of consumption. She then married an actor called Friedman and after him a Russian Baron. She once told Clare, 'Even if my husband asked me if I would be faithful to him during absence, I always replied, "Yes, for a fortnight", and he appreciated my frankness, and did not put me to the test. He knew that I was unable to prevaricate, and that I was a stormy petrel.' Eventually, despite being a Theosophist, the Princess found she could not bear the loneliness of widowhood and committed suicide.

In 1905 the Morel Beys attended the wedding of the Crown Prince to Princess Cecilie of Mecklenburg-Schwerin. Their stay in Germany came to an end in July that year. There was talk of Morel Bey being appointed Governor of Lebanon, but many doubts were expressed about the wisdom of his accepting. The most important reasons were his age and his poor health. But then Clare received an invitation to stay with friends in Lebanon. She decided to go in order to see whether it would be possible to face life in that remote and uninviting land. Thus in 1906, leaving Morel Bey to holiday in the Bavarian Alps, Clare and Lucien set off on the long journey across Europe.

Their first stop was Bucharest, where Clare had an audience with Queen Carmen Sylva. They had previously corresponded about the translation of some of her poems. The Queen told her: 'A holy, magical thing is work, the panacea for all ills, the only cure for nervous diseases, the only *real* consoler in grief.' Thence to Constantinople, where Clare called on Tewfik Pasha, the Foreign Minister, and brazenly suggested that she hoped it might be possible for Lucien to enter the Turkish Diplomatic Service under his guidance. During this visit Clare evidently had a vision in which she saw some ill fate overcome her husband in the Bavarian hills.

While in Constantinople, Clare and Lucien were given the chance to glimpse the Sultan, Abdul Hamid, when he visited the Medjidieh mosque. He had recently survived an attempted assassination. A bomb, heard by Clare on the day of her arrival, had destroyed fifteen carriages, and killed many horses and humans. The Sultan had remained his impervious self, raised his hand to forbid panic and in due course left the carnage 'unmoved, though pale of face'. When the Sultan came out of the mosque, Clare observed him closely:

> His face looked like a mask. Not a muscle of it moved. The mournful eyes scanned indifferently the countenances of the spectators assembled for the purpose of watching the auto-crat enter and emerge from the mosque, where he could commune with the One Being whom he considered above himself in power. I wondered what form his supplications took, or if the word were a misnomer.
>
> His face held all the weariness of people bereft of de-sires, because of their certain and immediate gratification. Ambition was perhaps the keynote of his character. To measure his own subtlety against the might of Europe, to hold at bay Powers with which he could never hope to compete in fair contest, occupied probably the intricacies of his mind.
>
> His secretiveness and craft certainly baffled the whole of Europe. He never put his cards upon the table. He realized that there was so little behind them that he would be shown up as the 'Sphinx without a secret', and the whole of his policy and power would collapse like the proverbial house of cards.
>
> Subsequent events proved that he was right in his surmise, and that to have kept afloat so long as he did was due to his genius for diplomacy, which has hardly been matched in history.

It was curious for Clare to glimpse at last the man for whom she and her husband had been working for over two decades.

Clare and Lucien made their way to Beirut via Samos, arriving there in July 1906. She cared little for what she saw, and decided that the best thing was to return early and finish her holiday with her husband, who was still resting at Kainzenbad. However, she was urged to visit Baalbek before departing and duly spent a night in a luxurious tent at a farm on the Plain of Horan. And she visited the ancient ruins of the sun-worshippers. On the journey back she called at Aley, where she was greeted by Eveline Drummond-Hay, wife of the Consul at Dar-al-Baida, bearing letters from Morel Bey, but also a telegram which announced his death. 'Of the hours that followed it is impossible to write,' continued Aunt Clare. But write she did:

> The world goes on remorselessly, whether one's dear ones are in it or not. Those who are left behind, still at the tether of life, feel as if the magnitude of anguish must inevitably fling them also forward, to mingle with the spinning atoms, in the vast Unknown.

The widow and son sailed from Beirut to Constantinople, where Clare was housed in the harem during the prolonged negotiations about her pension. It was the end of August before they were able to board ship once more and sail the rough Black Sea to Constanza. They then travelled by land through Romania and Austria to the Bavarian Alps.

After the obsequies, they returned to Berlin, where for the next year and a half Lucien completed his studies. Then in the spring of 1907 Lucien was appointed honorary attaché at the Turkish Embassy in London, and Clare was able to return to the land she considered home. The Turkish Embassy had moved from Bryanston Square to 69 Portland Place, and Clare took a small house in Devonshire Street. Mother and son were inseparable at this time; she clung to him in her grief, and it is impossible not to think that she overpowered him. In May 1907 her father wrote to his son Max:

> Clare is now settled, and seemingly to her satisfaction, as her little house is but a stone's throw from the Embassy, – is in the most aristocratic area, and 'just what she requires'. Lucien likes his work, the Ambassador takes kindly to him, and pushes him on, – so there is a hopeful outlook.

And in June he reported: 'Clare has been at the King's Drawing-Room, & Court Ball, being included in the party of the Turkish Embassy, at which I am very glad. She was rather fidgeting about it.'

Alas, old Mr Kappey was being optimistic. Clare soon realized that the wimpy Lucien was not cut out to follow his father's career. She feared he would be 'shipwrecked in the sea of ever-growing racial prejudice'. Thus the early years of their return were filled with anxiety: 'We hardly knew what to do for the best.'

8

The Indian Exploits of Major Max

Max Kappey, the father of Joan and Christian, and the youngest son of the family, was born at Chatham on 15 March 1868. He joined the Royal Marine Light Infantry as a Substantive in 1886, shortly before his eighteenth birthday. But his father found it too expensive to keep two sons in the British Army and so in 1897 Max was transferred to the 26th Regiment, Madras Infantry, in the Indian Army, where it should have been possible for an officer to live well within his means. Later Kitchener reorganized the Indian Army, and in 1904 Max's regiment was retitled the 66th Punjabis, and joined by what the military historian, Philip Warner, called 'a number of different peoples who otherwise would have had no hesitation in cutting one another's throats with or without a pretext'.

As a boy Max was judged to have a 'good moral character', a 'more than ordinary aptitude for mathematics', and 'an unusually retentive memory'. In November 1889, at the age of twenty-one, he sailed to India, where he remained far from family and friends. As he set sail he knew he would not see them again for five long years.

Fred came to see Max off on HMS *Malabar* at Portsmouth. 'I will not say much about my feelings as the ship was leaving the Dockyard,' Max wrote home, 'but they were not very lively.' On the voyage he shared a lower saloon deck cabin with two other officers who had been to India before and were able to give him a few hints about life out there. Max proved a good sailor, and enjoyed the sea air. He was amused by those who found the rolling of the ship difficult to stomach. As the sea got rougher, so the numbers on deck dwindled. There were various entertainments on board, a tournament of deck quoits, amateur theatricals, tableaux, cricket matches and deck games. There were also ladies on board, so after Port Said the ship gave some memorable dances. Most of the early voyage was calm, the ship cutting through the water and leaving a streak behind it like a stream of molten silver because of the phosphorus. But after Malta there were two exceptionally rough days when a storm raged, and Max was one of only twenty-nine out of a hundred that could still face a meal. The Suez Canal was a great disappointment, 'nothing but sand on either side as far as the eye could reach, with an occasional Arab running along by the side of the ship expecting money to be thrown to him'.

When they reached the Red Sea, the tropical heat hit them hard. Again, while most on board were 'more like wet rags than anything else', Max found the temperature 'only comfortably warm'. At length they docked in Bombay, and Max booked in at the Apollo Hotel. He presented himself to the Brigade Officer and found that he was to be posted to the 26th Madras Infantry, a native regiment, at Secunderabad, just north of Hyderabad. This was an exciting appointment, as Secunderabad was the largest station in India at the time, and deemed one of the best.

Max was met at the station by the Adjutant and found there were nine other officers, only two of whom were married. The Colonel, alas, was 'the most slovenly fellow I have ever come across, but the other fellows are very smart soldiers'. He lodged with the doctor until a bungalow became available. His first appointment was as second senior officer of the wing, which meant he would be mounted. The regiment had lately returned from the Third Burmese War, in which Upper Burma and its dependent Shan States were added to the Empire. They were occupied with two exhausting field days a week, and then a month living in canvas tents out in the jungle. Money was not a problem as Max had been sent over with an advance, and there was very little to spend it on anyway. His bungalow cost thirty rupees a month, shared between two of them. He found he could employ a butler for twelve rupees a month, a batman for five, and other servants for ten rupees in all. The most expensive item was the mess bill, which averaged 195 rupees a month. Nevertheless he still had 163 rupees of his advance, and 200 rupees left over from his first month's pay, so he was able to buy himself an Arab pony, which proved an excellent jumper. At first he found it curious to see 'nothing but blacks wherever you went & the majority of them nearly naked'. The worst problem was the insects: 'they simply fly round one's head all day long, some of them wasps as long as my middle finger. The mosquitoes do not trouble me as much as I thought they would but still I have been bitten about twenty times.'

Regimental parades took place early in the morning or late in the evening because of the intense heat of the day. On the anniversary of Queen Victoria's proclamation as Empress of India there was a parade of 9,000 troops at which the heavy battery of artillery was present in force, their huge guns drawn by enormous elephants. The elephants were well trained and were driven on by natives who gave them instructions by hitting them on the head with a large hammer and long iron spike. Troop exercises were demanding, as Max related:

There is no doubt about it that one gets real soldiering out here as there are huge field days every week out here & every time that the troops go out several men drop down & some of them don't turn up to another parade; but that is because they do not lead a healthy life.

Soon after this Max went on his first exercise camp, a gruelling experience. He went on ahead to pitch the tent:

It was rather lonely work being out in the jungle alone for two days but it was not long to be alone. On the 20th [January 1890] the brigade came out & the real hard work began. We used to get up at four in the morning & keep at man-oeuvres all the morning & afternoon & at night time we used to have night attacks. This lasted for a week & then war was declared against the other brigade.

We had some very hard days then & in the heat of the sun we used to march as much as 20 & 30 miles without food. On the 30th we had a very long day which knocked me up. We started at four o'clock in the morning & were fighting till three in the afternoon when we pitched camp at a place called Gutkasara, & we had only half got our camp pitched & had not had time to get anything to eat, when off we were ordered for outpost duty for the brigade. We went straight away & took up a position nearly two miles from camp & did not get back to camp until ten minutes past ten. Then we had to finish pitching our camp. We had nothing to eat all day; I had only two biscuits which I luckily put in my wallets; & at night it was fearfully cold on the ridge we were on after being in the sun all day. We were dead tired & had to get up early next day & the result was when I got in the sun again I was bowled over & got a touch of fever & had to be sent back to barracks. It was very slight though & only lasted for two days & I'm quite well again now although I'm not allowed to be out in the sun for long. A good number of fellows got bowled over, for we were out the whole day in the sun & now

59

it is pretty warm & goes up to 98 & 100 degrees in the middle of the day . . .

There is no doubt about it that this is the country for soldiering for we could not possibly have had harder work or longer marches in actual warfare. Two nights we slept out in the open without our camp being pitched. Then the country is so different; there is nobody to stop you & one can simply march where one pleases & camp where one likes. We went to several places & covered a tremendous lot of ground . . . We even fired ball ammunition one day. A lot of dummies were put up on a hilly position & then attacked by the whole division, artillery & all, numbering over 6,000 troops firing ball ammunition. It was a fine sight but very dangerous, one man of the 21st Madras Infantry was killed. How there were not more accidents is a wonder to me.

Max already spoke excellent German (obviously), and moderate French. But during his years in India he proceeded to learn some of their 225 languages, including Hindustani, Burmese, Punjabi and Pushtu, as well as Persian. He also qualified as instructor in the practice and theory of musketry. He became band president, and branched out unexpectedly into steeple-chasing and acting. As an actor he shone, receiving good reviews in the major Indian newspapers. One of them wrote:

Secunderabad is lucky to have such an addition as Mr Kappey to its dramatic resources. He played a difficult part brilliantly and with none of the awkwardness and shyness of a 'debutant' but rather with the finish of an old 'stager'.

His attempts at shooting were less successful as he never saw any big game.

Max remained at Secunderabad until July 1891 at which

point he was given twelve hours' notice to set off to Pokoku in Upper Burma, on the banks of the Irrawadi river. He was forced to cross India to reach Burma, a journey which took a fortnight because of an unexpected uprising in Manipur, which resulted in the murder of the British Resident and of the Chief Commissioner of Assam. Although this was swiftly put down, additional troops were on alert and Max thus took part in what is known as the Burma Campaign of 1891–2, the only action he saw in his military career. A fortnight after he arrived in Pokoku, Max was ordered to take over from a sick officer in Kan, which necessitated a long journey on horse-back, accompanied by a fellow officer. Bullocks pulled the carts, and the men had to swim two rivers, continuing their journey in wet clothes and sleeping in rest-houses or bamboo huts. The countryside changed to desert land, and then they crossed ranges of hills two to three thousand feet high. When it rained the roads became knee-deep in mud, making the work of the bullocks almost impossible. But it was a beautiful progress with ever-changing scenery and glimpses of the mighty Chin Hills 10,000 feet high in the distance. On his way to Kan, Max arrived at Gangaw with a hundred men and one other officer, where he had to stop as cholera was raging at Kan. There was nothing much to do as it was the rainy season, so the jungles were in too bad a state for troop move-ments. Max reported: 'The natives are quite quiet and will remain so till the rains are over.' In due course he was able to reach Kan. He found the Burmese very different in character from the Indians. They were less servile and had a better sense of humour. In Lower Burma the British were treated with great respect, while in Upper Burma the natives thought themselves every bit as good as a Brit. But in the jungle at Haka the Chins judged themselves better men, and Max had no doubt of it: 'They take care not to expose themselves much, but the way they surprise a column & then disappear in the thick jungle which covers the hills without leaving a trace behind is marvellous.'

A new problem confronted him. Despite the beauty of Gangaw with its views of the hill range on one side and impenetrable jungle on the other, it proved a hotbed of malaria (a disease which killed 30 million Indians a year). He was soon the victim of ague fever and dysentery. He found that just as he overcame it, he would go down with it again; this had an undermining effect on his long-term health. Clare, his sister, offered to write to Lord Dufferin (the former Ambassador to Constantinople and Viceroy of India until 1888) in order to get him moved somewhere more congenial. Yet like all good soldiers, what he hoped for most was the sight of action, and he resolved to stay there as long as his constitution allowed.

Out of the two months that Max spent up country, he was in bed for five weeks with fever or other jungle diseases. He returned to Pokoku in good spirits but with his weight somewhat down. His fate could have been worse. During the garrisoning of the four posts, three native officers and a hundred men died of fever. Cholera manifested itself suddenly and unpredictably. It worked fast, sometimes killing its victim within two hours.

Disappointment followed when the regiment was relieved due to sickness and loss of men and Max lost his chance of going 'on column'. He wrote to his parents:

It was crushing luck having to come down just as the cold weather was beginning and weak as I was I would have given anything to stop and have had a chance of really seeing a fight, as there is sure to be one with some of the tribes out there. I wanted to apply to go up again, but the doctor would

not let me go as he said I was totally unfit for any hard work
in the state I was then in . . .

His next post was Pagan, where he was in command of 230
men. The old town of Pagan was formerly the capital of
Upper Burma, and the religious centre. The town was completely surrounded by enormous pagodas lavishly covered
from top to bottom in gold leaf, but badly plundered. Max
found he was responsible for all decisions and that everybody
relied on him. However, after early parade, most of the day
was given to fishing and shooting. He stayed there until the
following August, then went back to Pokoku until January
1893. That February he went to Rangoon, where he gave
evidence in a court of inquiry. He was then seconded to the
Military Police at Katha and then at Mandalay. In July 1894
he was finally granted sick leave and sailed home to England,
where he stayed until February 1896.

9

A Bride for Major Max

Not long after his return to England in July 1894, Max met his bride. She was then living at 49 Castletown Road, West Kensington, looking after the young daughter of a Mrs Alma Watson.

Florence Lilian Mills, always known as Lily, was the daughter of George Jonathan Mills, described as a 'Gentleman', who lived in Norwich. The Mills family came originally from Hastings in East Sussex, their earliest known ancestor being one John Mills. Lily's grandfather, also called George Jonathan Mills (1820–1903), was an entirely self-made man, who amassed a fortune by shrewdness and perseverance.

By the age of thirty-six Mills had enough money to buy some land in Hastings, whereupon he engaged in a daring piece of speculation and bought Sir Morton Peto's land at Lowestoft in Suffolk. This led some members of the Mills family to settle at Eaton in Norwich. In 1867 Mills left Hastings and moved along the South Coast to Worthing for reasons of health. He established various partnerships, including the firm of Mills & Crome.

Basically he was a property developer, responsible for the development first of East Worthing, and later of West Worthing. As one of the West Worthing Improvement Commissioners he rebuilt Farncombe Road to a new concept, replacing the idea of a terrace of houses with detached and semi-detached villas set in their own gardens. No doubt in some quarters his activities were greeted with cries of horror, though his plans seem very moderate to modern eyes. The population of West Worthing rose considerably, and by 1894 the former spa was being described as 'chiefly a good-class residential area, with much the same relation to Worthing as that of Hove to Brighton'. Mills himself lived in West Worthing (then known as Heene) in a substantial house called Colville House in Gratwicke Road.

Mills was a generous man, deemed a public benefactor. He gave land for the building of St Botolph's Church and St George's Church. He moved Christ's Hospital to Horsham, and developed the land north of the railway station and at Durrington. When he died he was judged as follows: 'His career deserves to be cited as an illustration of rare perseverance, persistence, and foresight, and his influence must ever count an important factor in the development of the town.'

George Jonathan Mills died in 1903 at the age of eighty-three. He had retired to bed at about 10 p.m., seeming fairly well. But he grew restless in the night, and at about 5.45 a.m. was seized with a sudden spasm which produced syncope, leading to his death. He died a rich man, leaving over £129,000. His will revealed extensive ownership of estates and building plots, manors and messuages, with interests in real or leasehold hereditaments and premises. The ten-page document gave instructions regarding money invested in public stocks and funds, not only in the United Kingdom but also in India and the Colonies. There were debentures and debenture stock in railway companies, mortgage issuing companies, securities in county, municipal, district, parochial, local and other public bodies and authorities. He left complicated instructions as to how his active businesses were to be continued.

Reading this will and realizing the extent of old Mr Mills's fortune, it is sad that his great-granddaughters had so little to show for it. Why was there so little for them? The sum of £129,000 in 1903 would be the equivalent of about £3 million today. The problem was that old Mr Mills left too many heirs to share his fortune. He married twice, and inevitably the bulk of the fortune went to the second family – his second wife, four sons and two daughters, who remained well-off. Lily's father was the only surviving son of the first marriage to a girl called Jane, who died in 1872. Some money came to him, but then he married Jane Weston, and in turn produced at least ten children in the next generation, thus greatly reducing the share due on his death. On top of this, he was a profligate man, who amassed many debts, so much so that his daughters, Margaret and Dorothy, had to bail him out when they came of age. He lived until 1939, dying at the age of ninety-three, by which time all he had left in the world was £2,359.

Lily herself was born on 18 January 1871, and educated at the Leicester High School for Girls, where her conduct and industry were praised. From childhood her singing voice showed promise, and she made numerous appearances in Norwich as a teenage soprano. At the Church of England Young Men's Society Literary Class entertainment in April 1888, 'special mention' was made in the *Eastern Daily Press* of 'the singing of Miss Florence Mills, who displayed both taste and expression, and who received the only encore of the evening'. She also took part in amateur theatricals 'with sprightliness and spirit', often playing opposite her uncle, Arthur Weston. And she was a member of the Physiotic Society.

Lily was a slim and attractive 23-year-old, but not as pretty as her sister Jeanie, an aspiring opera singer, who had beautiful, innocent eyes. Max invited Lily to the theatre in November 1894 and she replied, 'I shall be delighted to go with you to

Drury Lane tomorrow & if you will call for me about seven, I will be ready.' Matters clearly progressed well, because by January 1895 Lily was writing:

My *own* Darling Max,

I am *so* sorry I did not write the same night that I arrived here. If I had known you were so anxious to hear from me, dearest, I would have written, but I thought *you* said you wd. not expect a letter from *me* every day. If *you* are as anxious to get *my* letters, as *I* am to have *yours*, I am sure you would like one every day, so will write. I find it *awfully dull* without you, darling, & miss *my kisses* very much . . .

Max and Lily were married at St Mary Magdalene, Paddington, on 10 July. Max's father, his brother Fred, and his sisters Stella Engelke and Clare signed the marriage register. The bride and groom then entrained for Worthing. In the years that followed Max often recalled the joy of that day: 'Our railway journey to Worthing – our collecting the rice and then our little episode on the sofa by the window & finally my coming in and seeing you with your hair down . . .'

On St Valentine's Day 1896 the Kappeys returned by sea to India, arriving in Belgaum, which was their home for most of the next three and a half years. Belgaum was a 2nd Class District commanded by Brigadier-General Reginald Hart, VC, who during his time there commanded the First Brigade of the Tirah Expeditionary Force in the North-West Frontier.* All the Hart family became friends of the Kappeys and they

* General Sir Reginald Hart, VC, KCB, KCVO (1848–1931). Sir Reginald's endeavours included forcing the Sampagha Pass and operations in the Waran Valley and the Mastura Valley, as well as in the Khyber Pass. A gallant man, he had undertaken numerous acts of valour before winning the Victoria Cross. He once jumped into the harbour at Boulogne to rescue a

were invited to dine sometimes several times a week. Lily became a special friend of their daughter Annie, who was nine years her junior, but who sadly died at the early age of twenty-two in 1902.

Lily was a popular addition to Belgaum life. She was soon acting and singing and in consequence breaking tough military hearts. Men asked for her photograph and she received semi-anonymous notes from admirers. After going to some lengths to explain how little he liked private theatricals, the reviewer of the *Magnet* enthused over a production of *The Pantomime Rehearsal* in which Lily played Miss May: 'Miss May's singing and Miss May herself . . . no wonder that the house rose and that bouquets were handed up in profusion.'

Max and Lily's first-born, Reginald Alexander Hugh, named after the holder of the VC, was born at Belgaum on 21 June 1897 after a difficult confinement. Known briefly as 'the Jubilee boy' in the regiment, his birth was the cause of much rejoicing amongst the fellow officers. Lily was just strong enough for chloroform and so avoided the worst pain of the birth itself. By the New Year Reggie's first two teeth had appeared.

Lily's diary for 1898 survives and from this emerges a picture of their way of life, native officers calling to give salaams, dinner-parties, musical entertainments after dinner. The path

---

drowning Frenchman, suffering severe wounds on the head and face when he landed on some sunken rocks. He won his VC for running 1,200 yards in a river-bed to rescue a wounded Sowar of the 13th Bengal Lancers. During his rescue of the Sowar, he was exposed to the fire of the enemy (whose strength he did not know) who rained bullets on him from both flanks and from the bed itself. He performed a successful rescue and drove the enemy off. Some years later he saved the life of a gunner who was in imminent danger of drowning in the Ganges Canal at Roorkee. While his principal enjoyments in life were big-game shooting and more or less all outdoor sports, he also produced a volume called *Reflections on the Art of War*.

of married life did not always run smooth, Max getting into a 'great rage' when he lost the way, or described as having been 'horrid all day'. He was prone to being rather jealous of his pretty wife.

In January Lily accompanied Max to Bangalore, where she was one of only three ladies. While he was occupied in varied military exploits, she was often left to walk with friends, shop and attend tea-parties. She had servants and an Ayah, but much of her day was spent looking after Reggie, her 'little man'. Intermittently Max suffered from fever, while Lily herself was often tired or feeling 'seedy'. Photographs of her at this time reveal a woman with a thin, drawn face, having swiftly lost her youthful bloom. She was pleased to be back in Belgaum in April. Presently they moved into a better bungalow, but Lily was 'rather sad at leaving our first home, & the house where my boy was born'.

It was no surprise if a dhobi-woman died suddenly or one of their friends suddenly contracted the plague and succumbed. A Miss Westbrook was fine until she caught a fever on a Friday. She was dead by the following Tuesday, and buried on the Wednesday. A frequent occupation was making small crosses for funerals. There was also bad news from home. Sophie, Max's sister, was ill again. In December Lily went down to the club with Annie Hart, who broke the news to her that Sophie was dead. 'Poor Sophie,' wrote Lily. 'To think we shall never see her again.'

Lily returned to England in time for the birth of her first daughter, Joan, at Southsea on 20 July 1901. Using the Unicode method of telegraphing she cabled 'Amuletum', which meant 'Confined this morning, *girl*, both doing well.' (There were some nasty alternative codes which were not needed, fortunately.) Max did not return to England until November that year, arriving by boat just before Christmas. The family were then in England until 1903. Christian, the younger daughter, known for some time as 'Baby', was born in Southsea on 31 January that year. Max went back to India alone soon afterwards, following a tearful port-side parting from Lily. He arrived in broiling heat in May, and, as he set off for Nowgong, he felt as though he was in a Turkish bath. He discovered that his fourteen-year-old saddle had fallen to bits and that moths had devoured much of his military greatcoat. Life was strange for him after such a long absence. The men in the regiment were mainly Punjabi Mahommedans, whom he found superior to the usual Madrassis. But he hardly knew any of the officers and found that there was no bungalow for him. Max had to lodge in a room in the mess, which was at least cheap living.

Lily stayed in England with her children, always referred to as 'the kiddies'. Hard times were already afflicting the family. The Indian life was one thing, the English quite another. Lack of money was becoming a serious problem, Max sending but twenty pounds home to cover immediate expenses and hoping that Lily would not have to use any of her own resources. She had some money from her family, having inherited £500 from her rich grandfather in her own right, whereas Max relied entirely on his meagre army salary. Then he was jealous if she told him that she had been escorted somewhere by a kind gentleman. He resented the fact that she wrote short letters while his were invariably several pages long.

Major Max was due to march to Peshawar, an envied posting, which he held between October 1903 and November 1905. He longed for Lily to join him, but did not want her coming through the Red Sea in August or September with two children (Reggie was to stay at school in England). Meanwhile the hot weather continued relentlessly, and he prayed for the monsoon, as he wrote to Lily:

It rained *hard* last night and as I was sleeping in the veranda, I had to get up and have my bed taken inside! It has been much cooler today but no clouds! so it was only a storm after all & *not* the monsoon. I wonder when it will really come as it is getting pretty serious and if it does not come within the next ten days there will be a famine in this part of India; already the price of butter & milk has gone up at the Cantonment dairy and I expect shortly that the price of horse's food will go up also! – If it does I don't quite know what I shall do as last month my balance of pay was 11 annas 6 pies and that was including my reward for Punjabi & after sending you your money half of which I had to borrow! This month I shall have none!!

The regt. is very expensive as all the funds had to be started afresh & also the mess & consequently the subscriptions are enormously high. – I don't see how I can keep from running more into debt until I have paid back government and it worries one dreadfully. – If we *march* to Peshawar the expense will be enormous and altogether I frequently get beastly fits of the union fever! I feel down on my luck now . . .

Presently Max was suffering from indigestion and a bad cough, but when the weather broke he soon felt better: 'Everything is damp & sticky & generally uncomfortable, but it is delightfully cool which compensates for a lot and I feel *much* better.'

Back in England, Lily was still living at Hamilton Cottage in Hamilton Road, Southsea. All was not well there; Joan had a fever and Lily was tired out looking after her young family on her own. She was miserable at the thought of leaving Reggie behind when she returned to India. After all, he was only six years old. 'It will, I know, be an awful wrench to leave him behind,' wrote Max sympathetically, 'but we must think of his future.' Reggie began his school life at Westbury House School, Southsea, where he appeared to make very fair progress. In October Lily sailed with Joan and Christian, an adventure for them, indeed the beginning of the most exciting phase of their lives. Luckily they did not realize the pressures under which their parents were living, the shortage of money, and the debilitating effect that India was having on their father's health.

Major Max frequently borrowed money – 2,000 rupees from a lending company in Poona, with monthly repayments of 100 rupees. His creditors treated him with the courtesy due an officer, though even in London there was never more than a few hundred pounds in his account. Meanwhile the parties went on, with invitations to meet General Sir George Wolseley, KCB, regimental point-to-points, dances, tennis and shooting parties, dinners at the club, and garden parties given by the Maharani Regent of Bangalore, and the Rajah of Kapurthala. At one gymkhana in May 1904 there was a mop tournament for teams of four, mounted on bare-backed ponies. The riders armed with mops tried to dismount the other riders by 'fair tilting and shoving'. Lily took part in a team tilting from traps, and there was a pig-sticking competition at which both the pigs and the spears were provided.

A highlight of this period in India was a performance of the comic opera *Dorothy* at the Garrison Theatre in Peshawar in March 1904. Lily inspired the local drama critic to write: 'Two new accessions to the amateurs in Mrs Kappey and Mrs Sangster, who played respectively as Lydia and Phyllis, are much to be congratulated on their graceful acting and sweet voices, and here one cannot pass on without saying that never has a prettier set of faces been seen among principals or chorus.'

Meanwhile Major Max was busy inventing things. With a

colleague he created a device known as the 'Mercer–Kappey Visibility Indicator'. However, this proved cumbersome and finally ineffective since anyone versed in the use of a slide-rule could apparently ascertain the required information in about ten seconds. During these years he was mainly at Peshawar, but commanded the 54th Sikhs at Chakdari, and served at Malakand and Dargai. In Malakand Lily suffered a bout of serious ill-health, which left her weak for a consider-able time.

As for the young girls dressed in their beautiful fairylike costumes, they were tended by friendly dark faces and sur-rounded by warriors in turbans. For the girls too there were endless parties, with masses of other children of the regiment to play with. The Kappey household consisted of six male servants and one nurse. At least on the surface their father looked well, handsome in his uniform, while their mother wore pretty long skirts and dresses. Each daughter had a be-loved pony, and Christian never forgot her father's magnifi-cent charger. They were to be lifelong animal-lovers, but in India they knew a style of life that would be etched for ever on their memories.

They had real-life mastiffs and goats to play with as well as their teddy-bears; there were picnics in the hills, and great sweeping views over hill forts, mountains and valleys. Their father created a garden, containing, as all Indian gardens of that time, many neat rows of flower-pots lined up like soldiers. Every now and again there would be a parade of turbaned soldiers, or the arrival of a great steam train at a seemingly deserted station. In England they would have shopped at Whiteley's; here they went to the general merchant's, a rough construction of wood and tenting, the roof held on with small boulders.

Their mother posed for photographs, one elbow leaning on

a stuffed tiger's head. Their father normally wore army kit and helmet, but sometimes emerged resplendent in his scarlet tunic, with sword and cross-belt. The family travelled about in a cart or wagon pulled by two oxen. Their house was full of elaborately carved dark wooden screens and photographs similarly framed. Everywhere there was a feeling of space and timelessness. Thus they lived for nearly the first decade of their lives.

In the middle of those years, which coincided almost exactly with the reign of Edward VII, there was a sojourn in England, Mrs Kappey taking her daughters back to Southsea in the early months of 1907. Major Max was left on his own, and presently reported a dream to his wife:

> I turned over and had another sleep and dreamt, sweetheart, that *you* were *with* me and then woke up to find that you were not there. But altho' it was only a dream, dear one, it was lovely and when I found that you were not there I wished it could have gone on & on. It is the *first* time that I have had a dream since you went, & I am so glad that I dreamt it was *you*, little woman. How plainly I saw you & how we *both* enjoyed it & as usual *you* would *not* be satisfied & I was only too willing to go on! – If it could only have been in reality, dearest . . . However, I suppose the time *must* pass and we shall have a right good time when I do at last come to you . . .

Reggie was at school at Eastbourne, so Mrs Kappey and her youngsters moved there from Southsea, taking a flat at 68 Royal Parade. Poor Reggie had been desperately lonely, so his tenth birthday was a great treat. His sisters saved up to buy him a special present of a photograph frame. Mrs Kappey sponsored it, so when they presented 2½d at the local store they were given a frame worth 9d.

Major Max took over command from a Major Prendergast,

who took three months' leave in Kashmir. A few days later the Kappeys' wedding anniversary came round, causing the Major to reflect on their marriage:

> We have been married now twelve years, little woman, and altho' we have had some quarrels, dearest one, if I had my life over again and *knew* what was to come, I would ask nothing better than to have it all over again. When you are away from me I KNOW & *feel* that you are the only one for me and altho' you have sometimes been jealous there has never been any cause for it. *How* I wish, dearest one, that we were together *now* so that we could live the day over together again. If you had your life over again, dear, knowing all you do now, would *you* also do as you did? I know you have had a very hard life, dear, as a soldier's wife, & we have always been hard up, but still at times we have been happy, haven't we?

Major Max was aiming to come home in November 1907, but his debts remained a seemingly insuperable problem. He wanted to clear them but there was no hope of doing so by then. He hated to owe money and he needed to replace his suit, shirts, collars and vests. Even his travel plans proved frustrating. He wrote to a shopkeeper called Dinshaw, hoping that he would store his boxes in Belgaum, but found he had retired from business. In the end he was convinced that he should return home soon by a series of letters from Lily making it clear that she could not cope with the arduous task of looking after three children single-handed, to say nothing of dealing with demanding landladies. As she seemed unwell, Max thought he should take her to see a specialist soon after he got back. In fact the only good news was that General (Sir Edmund) Barrow, commanding 1st Division, India, was pleased with the state of the regiment and gave Max permission to take his leave. The General confirmed this in a letter to

75

Major Prendergast: 'I was much pleased with the improvement in the 66th [Punjabis], not only had their physique improved greatly in the last year which is only natural, but there is a marked improvement in dress, bearing & general smartness, an improved tone all round.'

Major Max was granted a year's leave, and during his stay in England his old father died. The family returned to India on 9 November 1908 and went to Belgaum, where the regiment was once again posted.

During the next two years Major Max's health declined considerably. The years of Indian service had taken their toll, and this proved a worrying time for his family. In July 1910 he went to see his doctor, who began by telling him that his service was over, but then relented and said that after a few months' rest in India and a year or two at home he might be able to come back. Ever the optimist, Max noted: 'Hurrah! What did *I* say?'

However, in October that year Major Max's health again gave concern and he was granted eight months' sick leave. On 3 November the family sailed from Bombay aboard *H.T. Plassy*. But Major Max never reached home. He died during the voyage as the ship reached Port Said on 12 November. A fellow officer wrote to Lily to comfort her:

> The news came so suddenly & so unexpectedly that I have hardly been able to realize that we have lost a great friend & a much respected comrade; & I know the whole Regiment will feel the loss keenly. Words cannot express how I feel for you & the poor little kiddies, & I can only say that when my time comes I hope I shall be as universally regretted as he is.

Major Max was buried at sea, and for some years afterwards Lily asked others who passed by Port Said to throw a rose into the water in his memory.

Part Two

Coming Home

A friend of Joan's, who knew the family in their last decade and spent many hours talking to her, made the sad pronouncement: 'When they came back from India their life was over.' The girls were only nine and seven respectively, but there is more than a little truth in this depressing verdict.

Another friend, Betty Worthington, recalled that when Major Kappey died 'they were so badly off that they passed round the hat on board' to give Lily the wherewithal to get her family home. When the family reached England, Aunt Clare displayed her characteristic lack of kindness, as Miss Worthington has described: 'The aunt took both the girls and she dressed them in deepest mourning and sent the bill to Mrs Kappey!'

From then on life was to be a continuous struggle, one borne by Lily alone and then gradually imposed upon the daughters as they grew up. Once again I am able to know their plight in great detail from the papers left at Dargai in 1987. Sometimes in the preparation of a biography there are official documents and letters from great men; I have woven my story from odd scraps, old birthday books, decaying account books, notes written on pieces of paper, and of course letters too. When briefly I was researching an ill-fated biography of Diana Vreeland, her papers were hung about with the musky smell of expensive scent, fading but still strong.

Stephen Tennant's papers reeked of rose-water. The Kappey papers I was now exploring reminded me of spinstery old age and mangy cats kept indoors too long. But they revealed most of the secrets I needed to know.

Lily Kappey had numerous problems, not least the education of her son Reggie. Her main problem was money. Major Max died leaving £66.13s. 4d. in his will, and there were savings of £379.15s. 7d. at Henry S. King & Co. Lily had a little money of her own, and was granted a meagre army pension of £100 a year with small additions for each child. Whereas Major Max had latterly supported his family on about £450 a year while on leave, she had to subsist on £282 a year, based on the rate granted to widowed mothers with young children to support.

There were few things that were fortunate. However, Lily possessed the Freedom of the Fishmongers' Company and they were able to grant her some educational assistance for her children's schooling.

In April 1911 Lily settled with her children at the house in Clarence Road, named 'Dargai' after Major Max's Indian post. This was to be their home for the rest of their lives and at that time she paid £25 a year rent for it. In those days Clarence Road was not really part of Windsor but was in the village of Clewer, and it must have had a certain charm. This was before the First World War, and long before the terrible intrusion of urban development in the 1960s, when main roads and relief roads sprouted, a roundabout sprang up a few houses away and the old atmosphere dissolved.

The Kappey house at that time took on the aspect it bore until 1987. The way the house was decorated was essentially Mrs Kappey's creation and did not change fundamentally over the years. It was as I observed it in 1969, albeit in a somewhat run-down state by then. Gradually a variety of icons were placed in frames around the sitting-room. Major Max was the first. There he stood until the last day, in his handsome uniform, photographed and framed, and later, in one incarnation, hand-coloured.

Lily was fond of quotations and prayers. One such was 'Times change, and we with time, But not in ways of Friendship'. They retained friends from the Indian days and they made many new ones. One family they loved was that of Lieutenant-Colonel J. G. Anderson, the first of many Military Knights of their acquaintance. In his day the Colonel had also served at Peshawar. Now he lived in Salisbury Tower in Windsor Castle, with his wife and daughter, Trixie (sometimes known as 'Girlie'). His son John was in the Army, serving in Canada as a Private in the 27th Battalion (City of Winnipeg Regiment), 2nd Canadian Contingent. Old Colonel Anderson took a fond interest in the young widowed mother and her children.

Mrs Kappey was consistently generous to beggars who called at the door. Though she could ill afford the dispensation of bounty she never sent a man away empty-handed. Her life was devoted to her kiddies and to the memory of her dead husband. On anniversaries she placed a notice in the papers declaring that she was '*semper fidelis*'. Perhaps rather more worryingly, when Mrs Kappey gave her daughters a present she pretended it came from their dead father too.

Having survived the rigours of Indian Army life, Lily was faced all too soon with a new menace – the horror of the First World War. Her son Reggie was seventeen in 1914, and he had set his heart on a military career. Reggie's part in this story takes on more prominence at this time.

11

Reggie and Harry

Reggie's early life was not conducive to turning him into a lovable or easy character. Because his parents were away in India most of the time, he spent a good proportion of his childhood in England separated from them. He was often with his aunt, Jeanie East, at Kettering. Most of his communications with his father were sad little postcards: 'I do hope you are quite well & that you will soon be able to come home.' From 1903 to 1907, and again from 1908 to 1910, Reggie was left to fend for himself in a world of distant adults.

After school in Southsea, Reggie went on to St Bede's at Eastbourne. He was not particularly bright, but he tried to be industrious. He wanted to please his parents by getting into Wellington, and his headmaster did not think that this would be a problem. In the end he went to the Imperial Service College in Windsor. Colonel Anderson's daughter Trixie recalled him at this time as 'an attractive schoolboy of about fifteen'. From early on it was presumed – correctly – that he was destined for the Army; Reggie duly conformed to the inbred sense of duty of his father and followed his footsteps with neither question nor doubt.

In 1914, at the beginning of the First World War, Reggie was just seventeen years old, and was passing through the Royal Military College, Camberley. The pride of his mother and beloved by his sisters, he had also forged another friend-ship – with Harry Jacob (the soldier in the photograph taken with his mother in Joan's room at Clarence Road).

Arthur Henry Augustus Jacob was the son of Major Arthur Jacob, 20th Hussars, scion of an Irish landed gentry family, and Violet Kennedy-Erskine, a descendant of the Erskines of Dun, near Montrose, Scotland. The Erskines had enjoyed a long history, not devoid of incident. Two ancestors fell at Flodden, another was poisoned by his uncle in the seven-teenth century. Harry was descended from William IV through his great-grandmother, Lady Augusta Fitz-Clarence, the King's fourth illegitimate daughter. He was therefore well connected, being also a second cousin once removed of Prin-cess Arthur of Connaught (granddaughter of Edward VII). At Dun, Lady Augusta had laid out a garden with yew hedges and stone steps leading from terrace to terrace. By the time Reggie first saw it, its day was over. As Violet Jacob wrote, 'the trees that shelter it on three sides give it a tremendous solem-nity, and the associations that brood like a cloud of witnesses about it seem as much a part of its life as the coming and going of latter-day feet . . .'

Reggie was not a subtle or sensitive boy, but he had been raised in a house equally presided over by associations.

Harry's mother, Violet Jacob, was a novelist and poet better known in Scotland than in England. Her death in 1946 was marked by two obituaries in *The Times*. She was described as 'a natural writer, who soon revealed herself as an artist by instinct whose art satisfied without drawing attention to itself'. Most of her novels were set in the eighteenth or early nine-teenth century, and, though no longer much read, tell good, absorbing tales.

Having been brought up in the old House of Dun, in the Basin of Montrose, a haven for wild birds, that spot never quite deserted Violet, and even when far from home she remained haunted by it. Dun had been designed by the earlier Adam, and had one particularly beautiful room, the drawing-room, adorned with allegorical figures and plaster trophies.*

Like Reggie's family, the Jacobs had been stationed in India. Violet's diaries and letters from India† have now been published and it seems the family fared better than the Kappeys. Violet spent as much time as possible in the wilder parts of the country, studying indigenous Indian wildflowers, and painting them in watercolour. (These are now in the library of the Royal Botanic Garden in Edinburgh.) She was considered a gifted black and white caricaturist, and published her own poetry. One volume contained a preface by John Buchan: 'She has many moods . . . but in them all are the same clarity of vision and clear beauty of phrase.'

Harry Jacob, born in August 1895, was two years older than Reggie. His early years were spent in India, and his mother describes him throwing a football to the portly Maharajah Holkar of Indore, the latter's copious form adorned in mauve satin. Harry loved images of Hindu gods, loved to look at the temples; he drew well, and was, like Violet, a good story-teller. His mother related how he invented stories in a mixture of English and Hindustan at the age of four: '. . . he used native gestures and threw such absurd pathos into bits of his discourse that we had to hold ourselves tight in hand for fear of laughing and offending him'.

---

* The House of Dun was restored by the National Trust for Scotland and opened to the public in April 1989. Queen Elizabeth The Queen Mother called in for tea on 12 May that year.

† *Violet Jacob: Diaries and Letters from India 1895–1900*, edited by Carole Anderson (Canongate, Edinburgh, 1990).

Harry Jacob and Reggie met at the Imperial Service College, and were soon the closest of friends. For Reggie this was
an exciting friendship. Harry had all the things he might have
had, but for his mother's poverty. He used to take him up to
the House of Dun at Christmas, where they skated in 'the
Dish' with hordes of Erskine cousins.* The contrast between
this grand, almost feudal Scottish life and Reggie's own bleak
home life must have been acute.

Harry took their friendship more than seriously. In 1914 he
wrote a poem entitled 'Undying Friendship':

To R.A.H.K.

When alone I sit by this glowing fire,
And think of the days gone by
My heart is gripped by a great desire
Which makes me ponder and sigh.

Alas! that wish can never be gained
For it is that the past should return.
Nay! not *all* the past; it is too stained
But for the last three years I burn.

---

* Since this tale is full of curious characters, it is worth recording that one
of the Kennedy-Erskine cousins was Marjorie, who was fond of Reggie and
continued to run into him in Edinburgh long after these holidays. Sadly, she
suffered a mysterious end. In December 1934 she was found dead at the
Empress Club 'with a white scarf tied tightly round her neck and with a
large piece of blue stocking stuffed in her mouth'. The verdict was that she
had committed suicide while of unsound mind. The inquest recorded that
she believed herself under the spell of a dealer in black magic. The story
was never fully explained, but nor is it wholly forgotten in the Basin of
Montrose.

Years I have spent with one whom I love,
And shared all his thoughts and plans.
Ah! have I not prayed to Him above,
That again I may clasp his hands.

Together we worked at that dear old school
Together we played in its games.
All gone like the rising mist from a pool,
That is licked by these scorching flames.

I have no hopes of returning there,
For many a month to come.
P'raps never; I may not live to care
For my limbs may lie dead and numb.

I hope soon to be called to fight for my King
And shall go with a gladdening heart
I may ne'er return, but be borne on the wing,
Where one day we shall never part.

If I could but fight by the side of him
For whom I would give up my life.
The cup of my joy would be full to the brim
As we fought back to back in the strife.

If 'tis God's will that these eyes He has wrought,
Shall never more see him again
Of my mother and him shall be my last thought
Ere they number me out with the slain.

This prophetic ode gives a clue to the kind of friendship that existed between the nineteen-year-old Harry and the seventeen-year-old. In those days the friendship of Harry and Reggie would have been accepted in the spirit of comradeship, without the innuendo the present generation would inevitably accord it. Harry and Reggie themselves cannot have appreciated the homosexual nature of their relationship. However, the letters written by Harry to his friend leave little doubt in the modern mind.

When at the Imperial Service College, Harry came for lunch with the Kappeys every Sunday without fail. He called Lily his 'second mother', and he was fond of the sisters, who in turn adored him. Probably one of them, if not both of them, entertained the idea of one day marrying their brother's good-looking friend. Certainly Joan once gave their Sunday visitor the gift of a penny, prompting Harry to issue a gentle rebuke urging her not to spend her pocket-money on him: 'You must *never* do that again.'

In an emotional moment in November 1914, as Harry prepared to set off to the Front, the young Royal Fusilier wrote to Reggie from Guston, Dover:

How very happy your letters do make me, dear old chap, I do love them. Life is worth living when you say those kind of nice things to me, which you do not very often, although you always mean & think them, I know. I too look at your dear old face every night before I go to bed & every morning before I leave my room & LONG to be with you. It is always the *last* thing I do before turning the light out & before leaving my room in the morning, as regularly as my prayers in which I *never, never* forget you. Reggie old man, even if I am killed, it will not mean that we shall be parted for ever, because we shall one day meet in the next world if we keep straight & are not ashamed to follow God; & then, old man, NEVER parted, but live together for eternity. It is almost too wonderful & glorious to think of . . .

I have just this moment heard that the draft *is* going today & who knows I may be off too, but have heard nothing, will wire if so. Goodbye, dearest dearest chum, there is nobody in this world like you & there never will be; if I go think of me every day & pray for me. If it is God's will I should not return, well: always remember me as your dearest friend & the person who loved you more than anyone in the world except Mother & even then you are on an equal with her. Glad you liked the poetry; it is really just how I feel . . .

Tons & tons of love darling friend. Your ever *devoted* Harry.

On 7 December 1914, at 4.30 a.m., Harry crossed for the Front. He wrote Reggie another letter of an emotional nature, not long after bidding farewell to his mother:

. . . I feel sure, old Chap, that God, who is *so* kind, is going to take care of me for her & Daddy & YOU & *your* family . . . We are crossing by the Havre Packet Boat, as you know from my telegram; I expect that is the last you will know as to my whereabouts, as you know, no-one is allowed to say where they are . . .

Now Reggie darling, remember me always & pray to God for me & ask Him to let US get through safe & sound & meet out there and afterwards live happily together. Keep STRAIGHT dear Reggie, for the sake of Our Lord, Jesus Christ & for your *Mother's* sake & *mine*; above ALL keep yourself away from BAD WOMEN & when you come out, DO PLEASE take care of yourself & don't expose yourself unnecessarily & do all sorts of rash & mad things; remember how dear your life is to many of us . . .

The cross your dear Mother gave me, will always be round my neck & the photograph of you in the wee red frame is in its usual place & I hope, if I am killed, it will be buried with me. The photograph of you in the silver frame is in my rucksack on my back & if I have to throw the rucksack away, you may be sure I shall not let it go too, as I LOVE it

VERY VERY dearly. Goodbye, my own DEAREST CHUM, we have been great friends, haven't we & I hope we shall meet again & continue to be so ... Much love dear Reggie & KEEP STRAIGHT & be faithful to God.

Your ever loving, devoted chum Harry.

P.S. . . . What fun to think I shall soon be shooting Germans?

Harry did not expect to die but he did expect to be wounded: 'I am sure I shall not be lucky enough to escape *that*.' The following May he was back in England on leave, suffering some kind of trouble with his nose. He was stationed at Dover, and the nose prevented him being sent to Calais on special duty. Despite the war, his time there was filled with dances and when he was in London he managed various visits to the theatre. In December he spent ten days at the House of Dun on sick leave, with blood poisoning in his leg. He knew that at any moment he would be called back to the Front with the 4th Battalion of his regiment.

In June 1916, Harry wrote to Reggie from the BEF in France:

Dearest old man,

Just a line to say I may not be able to write for some time as there is a 'wind up' & we are moving but of course I can say nothing. I will write as soon as possible.

Goodbye dear old Reg for the present. Your devoted chum, Harry.

P.S. Let's hope all will be well. D.V.

Harry fell wounded at Bazentin-le-Grand, fighting in the Battle of the Somme on 14 July and died two days later at Étaples. He was a few weeks short of his twenty-first birthday. It is probably true that of all the soldiers who died so tragically in the holocaust of the First World War, he was one who was mourned the longest. His mother never got over his death. From that day on she wrote no more novels, though 'her inborn gift of poetry kept her creative genius alive'.*

In her desperation Violet relied heavily on those who had loved Harry. She never failed to remind Joan and Christian how much they all missed him severally and jointly: 'I know your poor little hearts do ache at the loss of your friend . . .' Sometimes the messages, no doubt delivered in kindness, have a worrying tone when read so many years later: 'Harry is happy so I am feeling happier myself. You must try too. He would hate to think of you miserable when he is happy.' From time to time she would send the sisters one of Harry's books. Where he had written his name she added an inscription 'With love from' above his signature. And she imposed her will on the sisters, urging them: 'He always took such care of me & you must take care of *your* mother too and help her always, like he helped me for he would love that.'

Mrs Kappey wrote to Violet Jacob, 'Is it really true that your darling boy is killed!! With so many praying for him I thought & hoped God would spare one of the finest boys that ever lived . . .' She signed it 'Your noble Hero Boy's 2nd Mother'. The Kappeys placed memorial notices in the paper for many years to follow, and Harry's framed photograph stood proudly in the front room until after Joan's death in 1987.

By the time Reggie heard the news he had been in the Army long enough to be unsentimental. He responded to the tragedy in a manner that was nothing if not blunt and matter-of-fact. He wrote to his sister on 24 July 1916 (mainly to apologize for forgetting her birthday): 'Fancy your big darling Harry being killed. Isn't it too awful to think about. I expect you are awfully upset about it.'

* *The Times*, 26 September 1946.

12

Reggie's Military Cross

A few weeks after Harry first departed for the Front, Reggie left the Imperial Service College with the headmaster's 'warmest wishes for his future success and happiness' and only a slightly crusty remark from the maths master, declaring that he had 'no notion of applying abstract reasoning to analytical work'.

On 17 April 1915 Reggie was commissioned as 2nd Lieutenant Land Forces, on the Unattached List for the Indian Army. A month later he was officially attached for duty to the 3rd Battalion, King's Own Scottish Borderers, and required to proceed forthwith to Portland. He was informed that the India Office would need him in October, at which time he would embark for India, though in the end he did not go to India but was transferred officially to the KOSB on 3 November. Reggie left his sad mother on 3 June 1915, presenting her with a summer rose which she kept all her life and which was still to be found in the house in Clarence Road in 1987.

After all their experiences, the family worried for Reggie. Aunt Clare was one who wrote to his mother 'to say how my heart is with you all, now that our dear Reggie is to join the brave army'. Clare prayed that God would watch over him and bring him home 'to you and us unharmed, and covered with glory'. Ever one to be melodramatic, Clare urged Lily to 'trust in God, who protects widows – as we have both learned to know'.

Reggie hated leaving his little sisters behind, and urged Joan to be a good daughter and to help their mother as much as possible. The young officer began his military life in camp near Edinburgh, 'in a valley where the wind whistles about strong enough to blow you over'.

Life in the King's Own Scottish Borderers was much to Reggie's liking. His companions were 'an awfully nice lot of fellows', who worked hard and played hard. Army life was stiff, to say the least. Reggie rose at 4.30 a.m., paraded from six to eight, then after breakfast inspected the lines and signed crime sheets all morning. He was on parade again between two and four, and six and seven. Mess was at eight and bed at 9.30. The routine was varied by a route march of twenty miles from 9 a.m. to 3 p.m. as often as three days a week. Part of this rigorous training for the Front included marching nine and a half miles to a trench and lying in it for two hours. This was often made more unpleasant by the trench being a foot deep in water.

Reggie remained in close touch with his mother, his 'darling Moss', and enjoyed 'a topping leave' with her in Cornwall. He was popular with his men. When he was bidding farewell to a platoon, one man made a short speech: 'You are the best sport I have met, Sir, and I wish that you were coming with us and so do all the others.' He witnessed the departure of 200 men for the Dardanelles, issued with topees and looking very fine as they marched down Princes Street in Edinburgh.

Reggie celebrated his nineteenth birthday in Scotland in June 1916. He 'demolished that lovely walnut cake & chocs', and wrote, 'I expect the war will be over quite soon now.' By September he realized that his prediction was flawed, and longed to see active service. He did not have long to wait. By

November he was serving with the BEF somewhere in France.

Reggie was a 2nd Lieutenant in the 2nd Battalion of his regiment. By May 1917 he had been appointed to an enviable job on Brigade Staff. In October he became Company Commander. His news from the Front to his mother at home was cheerful enough in its way:

> I am glad you rec'd helmet. You needn't be afraid of it as I didn't kill the man to get it but found it in a dugout in my objective. The man there didn't wait to be killed, he ran like a rabbit with several others. Of course we killed some while they were running away but I don't suppose the man with helmet was done in . . .

And there was better news yet. On 4–5 October 1917 Reggie took part in the Battle of Broonseinde, more specifically the operations at Polderhoek. He was commanding a support company in the early stages of the attack. The company lost their direction while advancing through a swamp under heavy shell and rifle fire. Reggie showed immense courage in getting the company heading back in the right direction and moving on its objective. They arrived at their destination, where he consolidated his position, in particular an exposed left flank. The company sustained heavy losses but Reggie's cheerfulness inspired all ranks with confidence. He also repelled several counter-attacks. His actions did not go unnoticed, as he reported to his mother on 2 November:

> Just a line to let you know the good news which has befallen me. This morning when I awoke I saw a chit beside my bed & on opening it discovered it to be from the Brigade Major congratulating me on my honour bestowed upon me. Moss I

have got the Military Cross – rather *bon* isn't it? Goodness knows what I did to get it but it was for the battle of Broonseinde on the 4/10/17 so they say. I could hardly believe it when I heard it, & I feel very pleased as you can imagine.

The assistant adjutant stood Reggie and the three other decorated men a dinner in a nearby officers' club. And his former commanding officer, Brigadier-General Linden, wrote to say, 'From what I hear of the fighting you are very lucky to be alive.'

At the end of the year Reggie moved to the Italian Front, which was freezing cold, and dull despite incessant bombing attacks from aeroplanes. He enjoyed a little leave in the summer before returning to the Front at the end of August. His war had further dramas to endure, as he wrote to Joan:

Well darling I have been in another scrap & this time I very nearly got a 'blighty one' as they call it. A shell burst a few yards away & a big bit hit me on the right foot. By Jove I thought my foot was off. I couldn't walk for two or three hours & now after 4 or 5 days can just walk very slowly. Yes I heard there was a rumour of peace being declared but of course it was not true. I think people who spread these rumours should be shot, as it causes all kinds of feelings especially out here. Anyhow old girl we are giving Bosche a rotten time & I hope it will be over soon.

By 28 November Reggie was able to report:

Yes isn't it top hole that there may be no more war. I think the old Bosche is pretty well beaten but one mustn't forget peace is not yet signed . . . We were in at the death, so to speak, & had great fun chasing the old beggar. It was pathetic to see the French people laughing & crying at the same time. The dear souls brought out coffee for us & in some cases came & helped us dig trenches. By Jove they were pleased to see us.

In March 1919 Reggie and his regiment made their way home.

13

Aunt Clare's Loss

Reggie was lucky to survive the war and to return with honour. Lily, who had suffered so much, thus fared better than Aunt Clare. Madame Morel Bey had spent most of the recent years engaged in London's social life, dabbling in the occult, and revisiting Berlin, Belgrade and Constantinople. By and large she cast a disapproving eye on the changing world.

Her son Lucien always accompanied her – her only solace in her nomadic existence. When travelling, Clare liked to buy small items from children, such as flowers, sweets or postcards, and, as she wrote, 'Sometimes, too, we broke the bread of friendship with a gipsy or two.' On the train journey to Constantinople, Clare was confronted by a gipsy who broke an egg on the ground and scattered poppy seeds on it. The old crone pronounced on the future, telling Clare she was destined for a restless life. Then she turned on Lucien.

> 'And *you*, Effendi,' turning her burning gaze on my son, 'your life's flame is leaping . . . up, and –'
> But I clutched my boy by the arm, and turned away with an impulse that forbade my listening any more . . .

Clare and Lucien returned to London, where, after serving for five years as Honorary Attaché in the Turkish Embassy, Lucien resigned from the service. Alas, the gipsy had not spoken idly. Clare concluded her memoirs on a sad note:

After the outbreak of war my son volunteered for the British Army and was called to the colours. But he responded to a Higher Call, and in the flower of his youth passed into that Silent Land where nationality and prejudice count no more, and where wars and rumours of wars have ceased.

How many mothers – who never forget – must now turn in freemasonry of grief to face a desolate world in this land of partings and meet the supreme problem of the great 'Why' . . .

Reading this sorrowful account of Lucien's end, we picture him in the trenches, sacrificing his life for the great cause, slain by the enemy in the field of battle. But no. Lucien died on 6 June 1916 at Clare's London home, 68 Warwick Road, of enteric fever. Described as 'the beloved only child and dearest friend of Clare Morel', he was buried in Brompton Cemetery in a prominent grave in the central area, where, in the fullness of time and after two more marriages, Clare would join him.

Deprived of her only real reason for living, Clare now devoted a certain amount of emotional energy to Lily's children. It is arguable whether or not her influence on their lives was a good one, but one thing was sure: they adored her.

Lucien was dead, and Harry Jacob was dead. So too died John Grant Anderson, son of the friendly Military Knight, Colonel Anderson. He was killed in action on the Western Front in October 1915. It fell to Trixie, the boy's sister, to break the news to Lily: 'His death was very sudden . . . caused by the enemy's shell fire. He is buried in a sweet spot . . . with 500 British soldiers who have laid down their lives for the Empire . . . When *will* this *cruel* war cease. We must try our hardest to be brave I suppose . . .'

To walk round Windsor cemetery today is to see the graves of other fallen soldiers, symbolic of so much manhood destroyed by war. I spotted another sad story – Lieutenant Hugh Poole, son of another Military Knight. He fell mortally wounded at Zillebeke, and died at Boulogne on 2 June 1915. He was twenty. Lily Kappey must have thanked God for the safety of her son, but presently she would lose him in another, wholly unexpected way.

14

Reggie in Peacetime

There were times when, to Reggie, peace seemed as exacting as war. In order to take part in a peace march through Edinburgh he and his men had to rise at 5 a.m., march two and a half miles to the station, twelve miles more in Edinburgh and then back, returning at 5 p.m. They had achieved what Reggie described as 'seventeen miles in the baking sun having been wet through once when we started'.

Following his wartime experiences, Reggie decided to remain a professional soldier. He served with the King's Own Scottish Borderers in Ireland and abroad, and in November 1923 the regiment went to India. During these years he was the apple of his mother's eye, and the surrogate son of Violet Jacob, who watched his development with pride and interest.

Reggie had stayed with the Jacobs in August 1917, during part of his leave. Violet reported: 'He was so nice, dear boy that he is. He is shaping to be a *fine* man. We were much struck with how he has developed, with such good sense & such a right & splendid way of looking at things. He is one of the best. I know that.' Violet often sensed Harry's presence: 'He is *so* near me often. Last night I was made so happy by feeling him beside me . . .' Deprived of her son, she was touched by Reggie's devotion to her. She recorded her joy when the war was over: 'Isn't that glorious to think he has come through safe? I can't think of any subaltern who has been out so long

99

who came through with his life. We must all be so unutterably thankful.'

All was well for a few years and Reggie continued to delight his family and friends. But then, to his mother's horror, he formed a most unconventional union. On 10 April 1926, at the age of twenty-eight, he married in Plymouth a widow considerably older than himself. His bride, who gave her age as thirty-seven but was in fact forty-six, was Mrs Kathleen Molony, always called Dolly, the daughter of a deceased Irish journalist with the far from exclusive name of Charles Ryan. To make matters worse, she was a Roman Catholic. Little is known about her early life, but her arrival in Reggie's life broke Lily Kappey's heart. No Kappeys attended the wedding.

Lily can be forgiven for feeling let down. She was a young widow, and she loved her son. He had survived the war and other dangers, and now he was lost to a woman eighteen years older than he. Her Victorian attitudes and her conventional life with the Indian Raj had not prepared her to handle the situation with either mercy or tolerance. Even in her diary she would write of 'Joan, Christian, *and their brother* . . .'* For a time she did not feel able so much as to mention his name.

Interestingly, Joan and Christian (but particularly Joan) were fond of their unconventional sister-in-law. Dolly had known Reggie for some years before the wedding, and a few of her letters to Joan survive from 1923, at which time Reggie was serving in Alexandria. These portray a solitary woman seeking peace in an hotel in Cork, and not always finding it. She wrote affectionately of 'Reg', as she called their brother, and was busily knitting socks for him. She decried the way

* On 17 June 1932, Mrs Kappey noted: 'Chris off to Scotland to stay with her brother!'

that tourists had overrun her beloved Ireland, and even wrote, 'I think I'd rather have the gunmen about.'

Following his marriage, Reggie effectively left the story of the two sisters. As we shall see, his voice is only heard expressing itself with a certain disdain about the way the two sisters were treated by the men they loved in later life, Dick Bonham and Major Clough. But what fate befell Reggie and his wife of advanced years?

The Second World War found Reggie based in Edinburgh, but presently he set off to East Africa, where he lived for the rest of his life. In 1944 he and Dolly parted. It is not known exactly why, or what Reggie's mother and sisters thought about this. There survives an uninformative letter from Reggie to Mrs Kappey, written in his latterday brusque tone:

> A letter from you some time ago. A little surprising to hear your comments about Dolly.
>
> I still have Joan's & Chris's letters in which they say they cannot understand how I stuck it so long. The break was coming slowly but inevitably & now it has come there is no going back, rightly or wrongly. I am sorry for Dolly but she has brought it on herself & not for want of telling. Three times I told her I'd go if she didn't mend her ways & up to the time I left we could not see eye to eye. To change the subject I hope you are better now & that these b——y bombs are not worrying you too much . . .

I do not know which ways Reggie thought that Dolly should mend and it is dangerous to speculate. If she had succumbed to a vice the most likely one is the bottle. She was then sixty-four years old, and unhappy with Reggie. There is certainly evidence that Reggie himself had a spell on the bottle, though he later eschewed all alcohol. None of the other members of the family ever hinted that Dolly had any kind of vice, though Reggie's drinking was mentioned in letters.

As soon as Reggie and Dolly separated, Mrs Kappey changed her ideas and supported the deserted wife; such is the wayward way of a mother who no longer feels her son is threatened. Dolly also remained in touch with Joan and Christian, and once a month until she died she wrote to Reggie with her news.

During the late forties, fifties and sixties Dolly lived at Iden Manor, at Staplehurst, near Tonbridge, a heavily gabled residential home for ladies, founded in 1935, and run by Catholic nuns. It was set in an extensive park, and had a large conservatory attached to it. Dolly went there because her sister, Nora, had been treated as a patient in their alcoholic unit and she was impressed by the place. Dolly lived at Iden Manor as one of their elderly residents. Here Mrs Kappey stayed with her in 1951, reporting to her daughters: 'Have the room the Duchess* always has when here, just going to have tea with Dolly in her room. She is wonderful & sends much love.'

Dolly died at Iden Manor at the age of eighty-nine in November 1969, leaving Reggie £500, and £100 each to Joan and Christian. Presently Joan wrote to ask the sisters if they knew anything about Dolly's early life. The Mother in Charge replied:

Mrs Kappey was always very reserved about her personal & private relationships, & did not discuss her family affairs with either Mother St Angela or myself. Of her first husband we know nothing, & certainly there were no Irish relatives (that

* The Duchess of Wellington (the poet Dorothy Wellesley, 1889–1956) retreated here from time to time. Her friend Vita Sackville-West wrote of her: 'Her health, never very robust, had considerably deteriorated and only her natural courage kept her going.'

we knew of) to inform of her death. She kept her secrets to the end. She was intelligent & relied on her own resources for business affairs. She worked at crossword puzzles to the very day of her death. She was truly valiant & a very brave woman.

Dolly is still remembered at Iden Manor and is buried in the grounds. As for Reggie, he remained in Africa. He remarried sometime soon after 1944 a wife called Eileen. He appears to have lived reasonably happily, if frugally, first in Kenya and then at his home, Doon, about forty-five miles from Gordon's Bay in South Africa. Very occasionally he visited England, and like other favoured guests of his sisters he was photographed standing in the garden by the wall against which Dick Bonham was photographed.

Reggie predeceased his sisters, but we shall meet him again before the end of the story.

15

Joan and Christian at Home

The cast of characters residing at Clarence Road consisted of Mrs Kappey and her two daughters. None of them worked, and it is indeed hard to imagine how they survived at all. In 1915 Mrs Kappey wrote to say that her income was '£257 wherewith to keep & educate my two daughters'. In 1928 her tax return gave her annual pension as £195.

Obviously I never met Mrs Kappey, who had died some years before I met the two sisters. Most of what I know of her is from the papers she left behind. But in the summer of 1995 I went to see a somewhat younger friend of the Kappeys, Miss Betty Worthington, whose family had moved from St John's Wood to a house in New Road, near Clarence Road, in her childhood.* Thus she met the Kappeys. She was not sure what she thought of Mrs Kappey. She admired her courage in bringing up the young family single-handed. On the other hand Miss Worthington described Mrs Kappey as 'always the memsahib', who referred to her daughters as if speaking of slaves: ' "my girls", she used to say'.

Miss Worthington recalled that Mrs Kappey 'wasn't very nice to them', though they were devoted to her. Once she looked at Miss Worthington's new car rather disapprovingly.

---

* Miss Worthington's home was later demolished to make way for the roundabout on the Windsor relief road.

The Kappeys could not afford such a luxury. Mrs Kappey commented, 'Of course my girls have their *bicycles*,' as though that was somehow better for their characters. Chris never had a room to herself. She slept in the same room as her mother. There were other unnecessary divisions and jealousies. Miss Worthington recalled a grim afternoon:

> When they were giving tea once, they were all there and Joan was pouring out the tea, and Mrs Kappey suddenly said: 'Joan. Who's pouring out? Are you pouring out or am I?'
>
> Mind you, they had a terrible time. Because when they landed, they had the room upstairs as a schoolroom. And they never had any money, really and truly, and they used to share the governess with the vicar's children.
>
> But Mrs Kappey really was a so-and-so. She thought of nothing but herself.

Another friend of the family, June Bourne-May,* confirmed this view: 'They were totally dominated by "Darling little Mother" as they referred to her. She was anything but a darling and wouldn't allow the girls to get jobs and lead normal lives. They had to be at her beck and call all the time. Everyone in Windsor felt very sorry for them.' All her life Mrs Kappey was brought her breakfast in her room by one or other of her daughters. She ran the house as if it were fully staffed.

While Reggie had been given a good education, the two sisters were rather inadequately educated. Joan was a pupil at Oaklands in Birkenhead for a while, and Chris at Eastbourne. Mrs Kappey did a certain amount of entertaining, especially

* June Josephine Peake-Cottam, wife of Geoffrey Bourne-May, Coldstream Guards (1921–88).

as the girls grew up, when soldiers from the barracks were regular guests at the house. And she would send them to parties, accompanied by a maid in a dark blue dress, found for the occasion. Miss Worthington's particular friend was Chris: 'Little Chris was very attractive. She was a pretty little thing. She should have married. Poor Joan never had a chance really as she wasn't a bit attractive.'

Every now and then one or other of the sisters left Clarence Road for a spell, but in due course they always returned. While they were away, they sent postcards every day, these cards illustrating a cute puppy or a pair of enchanting fluffy kittens. It was a situation that would see each one through to death, Joan being the ultimate survivor, living there for seventy-five years. Mrs Kappey had a particular way of making them feel guilty while they were away and she was forever reminding them that there was work to be done when they returned. This was wrapped up in messages concerning their wellbeing, but the sense of guilt they should be feeling was always transmitted.

A typical letter was one written to Joan by Mrs Kappey when she herself went to Norwich to stay with her brother:

A few hurried lines to say I rec'd no P.C. this morning as promised which much worried me, so wired you & was thankful to get the reply that you were alright! as hate the thought of leaving you alone, dear . . . Am glad you are enjoying yourself & letting house go, *don't* bother about it . . . Fancy Giles turning up at that hour to see you, how sweet!! but naughty at the same time . . . It will be nice to be able to see daylight through the windows on our return! but *why* did you do them while we are away dear, it is too much . . .

Despite Miss Worthington's fears that Joan had never had a chance with men, there were a great number of love letters amongst her papers. They were tied up with ribbons and had been faithfully kept. It was to these that I next turned in my quest to understand Joan better.

16

Fond Friendships

I could not escape feeling a sense that I was invading Joan's privacy when I began to sort the letters that had come from the various boyfriends. It was also hard to be sure to what extent some of them were actual boyfriends. Most of them came into her orbit by being friends of Reggie's, and as the First World War was raging and many of them were stationed overseas, or serving at sea, she struck up correspondences with them, some of which lasted for years.

As we know, Mrs Kappey invited officers to the house to meet her daughters. In later life, Joan told a friend and neighbour that the young men were often more bewitched by her mother than by her.

The first five friendships were more in the nature of loving friendships than love affairs. It was interesting to read the ways in which the men expressed themselves and to learn how they coped with the grim exercise of serving in a war in which they might be killed at any moment. The philosophy of that generation was wholly different, and sometimes it was not even philosophy but a kind of numbing of the brain and of the sensibilities in order to operate as part of the war machine.

The first boyfriend sounded a kind and sympathetic character, and it is clear that Joan's letters to him (which do not survive) gave him comfort while he was away. It is also clear that he was genuinely fond of her. The correspondence lasted some four years.

The Sailor: Jack Head

In June 1915 Mrs Kappey took her daughters to Mevagissey in Cornwall for their summer holidays. This proved a more than memorable holiday, almost certainly one of the truly happy times they all spent together. There they met Jack Head (J. S. Head) and his brother Arthur, who were staying with their aunt at St Ewe Rectory. They were nice friendly boys; the younger one, Arthur, was still at school at Bromsgrove, while Jack was at the Royal Naval College, Keyham in Devonport, training as a midshipman.

Jack and his brother lived part of the time with their grandparents at 2 Clarinda Park East, Kingstown, Co. Dublin. During this time their parents were living in Africa, where Jack's elder brother died. And not long after the Heads met the Kappeys, Jack's sister, 'a dear little golden-haired girl', whom he had not seen for six years, died there from appendicitis. At the end of the following year his old grandfather died, so he was often quite lonely.

The summer holiday of 1915 was, however, a great event in all their lives. Jack looked back on it with abiding delight: 'I wonder whether we will ever have such fun again as we had at Port Mellon' became an almost constant refrain in his letters to Joan. Previously he had thought himself rather a dull chap and was thus more than touched that Joan showed any interest in him at all.

They all chased each other round the beach, splashing in the sea, and enjoyed pursuing each other with seaweed and jellyfish. Joan was fourteen and still young enough to run about with bare brown legs. In a moment of lyricism, Jack described the scene to her: 'I remember those little brown legs of yours, all sunburnt, running across Port Mellon beach as fast as any fairy or sea nymph . . . I think you are much nicer than any fairy or anything as fragile, and very pretty.'

One afternoon Jack rowed her and Christian over to Ash for tea. Another day they went fishing and Joan caught her first mackerel, a huge one, and shortly afterwards her first chad. Then one Sunday evening, after church, he and Joan went off secretly together and no one knew where they had gone. Jack took her for a ride on his motorbike, regretting only that it was too foggy to see much. Jack gave Joan a sweet-pea flower and was delighted when she told him later that she had kept it.

Likewise, on the way back in the train Joan gave her new friend a piece of heather and he put it in his cigarette case to keep it safe. He used to take it out from time to time to remind him of Joan and the happy days. Presently there was an exchange of photos. As was her custom with those she loved, Joan put her picture of Jack into a frame, while Jack in turn looked forward to displaying her image on the wall of his cabin.

This friendship was forged in wartime and soon Jack was back at the Naval College in Devonport. He found his work interesting, and was proud to be appointed one of eight cadet captains amongst sixty boys. He enjoyed playing rugger and hockey. In rugger matches he relished a really muddy game, and emerged looking like a miner after a day in the pit. Nor did he heed danger. In one match his right forearm was crushed and he had to keep it in a sling for several days. At the theatre an old lady observed his wound and said in a loud voice, 'Look at that poor Kidy [sic] from the Dardanelles.' Jack hoped to be showered with bounty, but nothing happened; the experience was more embarrassing than anything else. He was clearly an active rugger-player. In a subsequent match he was hurtling towards the touch line when he was collared, falling onto the touch-line flag. A five-inch splinter entered the knee just below the kneecap, and he was dispatched to hospital for a week.

At night Jack slept in a hammock about five feet above the ground. He found it perfectly easy to sleep there once in it, but almost impossible to get into. Invariably, when he tried to climb in, he lost his balance and tipped himself over the other side.

Like all good sailors he longed to go to sea: 'I hope I will get out in the first lot and if we get leave before we go, I shall move heaven and earth to see you.' Joan said she would pray for him, and he wrote in reply: 'Whenever my turn does come to go to sea it will help a great deal to know that you are praying for me and I only hope I will be worthy and do my duty. I will only think myself lucky to be able to serve God and my country.' Joan then sent him a little cross to protect him from being blown up by a mine, and he assured her he would wear it always. He genuinely loved receiving her letters, and at each post went to see if there was a letter for him.

After the death of his sister, Jack besought Joan to be 'a little sister in her stead', a sentiment both touching and slightly disappointing. Reading the letters years later, I got the impression that sometimes he was a suitor, and sometimes he preferred to be an honorary elder brother. He passed out of Naval College four places higher than when he had joined the Navy. After some leave, he joined the 1st Battle Squadron, HMS *Vanguard*, a dreadnought, as a midshipman in February 1916. He was 'wild with excitement' at the prospect of spending several days with Joan at Dargai. Every morning the two sisters and the dog, Gipsy, came into his room to wake him up.

One evening he and Joan went to see *Red Riding Hood* at the Theatre Royal in Windsor and afterwards they walked home, taking a circuitous route in order to spend longer together. Nevertheless Jack wished the walk had been longer still: 'I was quite content to be piloted by you.' Back at Dargai they would sit up late listening to gramophone records, a particular favourite being tunes from the famous revue, *The Passing Show*.*

When Jack's leave was over, Joan came with him in the taxi to bid him farewell, and Jack paid for her ride home. Naturally Joan felt low, and she was not well. Jack tried to cheer her up in the idiom of the day: 'Buck up old girl and don't let that cold of yours be aided by low spirits. If I was there I might help you to get rid of it, at least I would have a very good shot at it.'

Aboard *Vanguard* Jack slept on deck; there were severe gales, and he was more often cold than anything else. The gun-room was no sanctuary if seasickness was to be avoided, as the ship had a particularly nasty roll. Generally they went through 'some rough times', experiences that turned Jack from boy to man. As for recreation on board, they had two gramophones and a pianola; one much-played record was a selection from *The Passing Show*. Most of all he looked forward to receiving letters. Signing off, he would write: 'Lots of love and a kiss to yourself from Jack. P. S. You will have a lot to claim when I next see you and I shall also claim my full amount of kisses.' This was a bit more encouraging.

Jack wanted Joan to teach him the piano so that he could play in the mess; he made some progress on his own, but did not think he would 'get any further than strumming by ear'.

---

* *The Passing Show*, a revue by Arthur Wimperis and P. L. Flers, with music by Herman Finck, first opened at the Palace Theatre in London in April 1914.

He was also training for a boxing match on board *Vanguard*, which took place in May: 'Your Knight managed to get into the semi-final and then got laid out in the second round. He however won a topping silver cigarette case.' Soon after this he was competing in a sailing race in a cutter with another midshipman.

On 31 May 1916 Jack saw naval action for the first time. He took part in the Battle of Jutland. It seems extraordinary to have it described as though it was a game:

> We have at last had our Baptism of fire. We met the destroy-ers and cruisers and battle cruisers of the German Grand Fleet about 4 p.m. on the 31 May. We engaged them for the rest of the evening until about 7.30. We did not see any more of them until about 9 p.m. when their destroyers made a torpedo attack on us and got driven back. Our destroyers gave them a very hot time.
>
> We sank a good many of their destroyers and cruisers. The old *Vanguard* did for a cruiser and destroyer herself. I shall never forget seeing the cruiser hit. A line of flame the whole length of her and she then slid down. It was a wonder-ful sight seeing our shells burst. A huge crimson flash.
>
> We did not see the Germans after 7.30 until it was quite dark. They then had their torpedo attack. The whole hori-zon was lit up with their firing. We did not see them again after 10.30 p.m.
>
> I am sure you would have enjoyed it all. We have at last got what we have been waiting for for ages and I wish we had more of it. I wish we could have had it out with the whole lot.

This cheerful description gives no hint that the Royal Navy lost more ships than the Germans did in the battle, though they did force the enemy to retreat. Soon after this, Jack saw another memorable sight – the remains of the *Invincible*, 'in half, and twisted badly'.* Undeterred, he wrote on 15 June: 'We are always hoping that we will get at the Germans again and end the whole thing. It is simply awful only half doing it and not being able to get them properly.' He looked forward to the day when they had 'abolished the German Navy'. He wrote optimistically in July 1916: 'I am certain that it won't be very long now till we are laying out the Germans once and for all.' Meanwhile Joan had been knitting Jack a long scarf, which thrilled him. He wore it every morning for many years, while rowing in the galley, and thought of Joan at Dargai knitting by her fireside.

As so often in wartime, long dull periods followed those intense, exciting and frightening moments of action. In August the crew of *Vanguard* enjoyed a review on board another ship, the *Monarch*: 'You would not believe what good-looking girls "snotties" make.' It was about this time that Harry Jacob was killed. Jack commiserated: 'It is most awfully sad about your brother's chum being killed. I can sympathize with all because I know what it is like.' This was expressed with rather more understanding than Reggie had been able to show.

Joan spent the summer holiday of 1916 with her mother and Christian in Eastbourne – enjoyable, but lacking the zest of Mevagissey. Jack's days of seven-week leaves were past, and even when he did have leave he had to spend time with his grandmother, or at the Rectory in Cornwall with his cousin, who had been badly wounded in the war and was recuperating there with his family. Jack's visits to Joan, still eagerly

---

* King George VI, serving as a junior officer in the Navy, also saw the shattered wreck of the *Invincible* at this time. Admiral Hood and 1,026 of her crew had died.

sought, were often rather hasty, squeezed in between arrival in town and a rushed departure on the midnight train west.

Jack was a pretty regular letter-writer, though not as regular as Joan, and he often apologized for replying late. As he grew older he adopted a jaunty tone at times, incorporating the phrase 'By jove' into his prose: 'By jove Joan we have every hope of getting our leave a little earlier this time . . .' In October Jack sent her a small memento of the Battle of Jutland, a piece of metal for her to wear on her bracelet. He promised to buy her a new bracelet on his next leave, and charmingly always included her in his plans.

October 1916 found Jack at sea in wintry weather, bringing with it a moment of respite from war: 'The weather is blowing up a bit now so I think we will be left in peace by the Bosches but of course they might take it into their heads to come out but I think they won't face "mal de mer" as well as us.' In the interval Jack thought up a rhyme for the 'right person' to receive at Christmas:

> To our friends who cannot greet us on the sea
> To our foes who will not meet us on the sea
> This message both may ponder,
> Till they hear the guns out yonder
> Absence makes the heart grow fonder
>   Wait and see.

Jack added: 'This of course is written so as to apply to one person and I don't think you will find it hard to guess to whom I refer . . .'

Jack's letters began to make tentative plans, months in advance, concerning what they would do when he had leave. He invariably suggested a visit to London and a theatre. It helped him get through the long months at sea to dream of homecoming. The actual meetings were, of course, depressingly short and infrequent. Jack packed in a lot when on land, with visits here and there: 'We have a lot to do in a very short time although I would be quite content to sit in front of the fire yarning to you for the whole of my leave but I am afraid Gran and None [the wounded cousin] would have some words with me on the matter.' At Christmas 1916, Jack only managed to see Joan for one afternoon, with a visit to a rather unsatisfactory show, *Razzle-Dazzle*.*

In 1917 Jack's letters began to grow a little distant. He was transferred to HMS *Monarch* and in November he was promoted from being a 'snotty' to a 'pukka' Sub-Lieutenant. The next month he moved again to be second-in-command of HMS *Crocus*, a minesweeper. It was at this time that Jack began to press on Joan the title of 'adopted little sister'. He thought back with great happiness to earlier times and was sentimental at the thought of sitting in the front room at Dargai, playing gramophone records. But he was growing up and had responsibilities. Sometimes the long months at sea wearied him. He got tired, he wrote in September 1918, 'not exactly of the sea but of the incessant joy of watching for Fritz'.

Presently he was writing of a Christmas leave in Ireland and how he had hidden some mistletoe in a cushion, surprising various girls 'who all thought what a polite Naval Officer but very soon realized that it was not so polite after all'. Joan wrote back describing him as a 'hardened old seafaring person . . . with a girl at every port'. Jack responded: 'I am quite sure girls or most of them would not be bothered with such an imbecile as myself, Joan.' Just before the war ended,

---

* *Razzle-Dazzle*, a revue by Albert de Courville, Wal Pink and Basil Macdonald Hastings, had opened at Drury Lane the previous June.

Jack was promoted Lieutenant and in his last surviving letter to Joan, he wrote: 'Yes, I think I will stay on in the service.'

I have not discovered what happened to Jack. At a certain point he sailed out of Joan's life. He sounded a nice, kind person, and had the war not taken him away, perhaps a romance could have blossomed. Their friendship was sustained by her kindness and devotion, nurtured mainly by letters from when she was fourteen until she was eighteen. Reading the letters today is a sad experience, because the friendship led nowhere. On Joan's side, at least, there was real affection and loyalty. But it was a dead end, and there were to be more of them.

The Fusilier: Arthur Head

There are some equally friendly letters from Jack's younger brother, Arthur, then a schoolboy. He was almost certainly too young to be considered a true suitor, but he was affectionate. He too recalled the fun of the Mevagissey holiday. 'You say in your letter that you hope I miss you a wee bit. I should think I do miss you, I miss you an awful lot, but I can't express my feelings. When you went I felt I could hug you on the platform, only I couldn't.' At school he was sustained by the kindness of her letters, by pieces of ivy sent in the post, and he asked for a photograph.

After leaving school in 1918, Arthur applied to join the Indian Army but was told that they were taking no more officers. Instead he joined the 3rd Reserve Battalion, Royal Dublin Fusiliers, finding himself stationed at Weelsby Camp, Grimsby, an 'awful hole'. Thereafter he too drifted from the scene.

From this stable there came also two other friends, Jack Preston and Jock Martin.

The Airman: Jack Preston

Jack Preston came from Bedford, and was in the Army in 1918. He too had been on the Mevagissey holiday, and, like young Arthur, had longed to join the Indian Army. But his father told him it was now 'a refuge for the destitute' and that it admitted 'a great many natives', as a result of which Jack 'could never entertain a wish now for that arm of the service'. He therefore became an early recruit to the newly-formed Royal Air Force and the beginning of 1919 found him stationed in Salonika, engaged in sports and waiting to know if he would be sent home to England or on to Russia.

Jack was fascinated by flying and reported that 'the Handley-Page which landed at Karachi with Gen. Salmond* caused great consternation. The natives had of course never seen an aeroplane before, and it was evidently a great novelty for them.' In February 1919 he commented: 'At present the RAF is a one-eyed show as they are accepting anybody and naturally there is a great deal of riff-raff. However I still like flying very much.'

Jack Preston's friendship with Joan was progressing reasonably well until he made a grave blunder. He offended Joan by inquiring about her age, and though he apologized, his letters ceased thereafter. But he sent his photograph.

---

* Marshal of the Royal Air Force Sir John Salmond (1881–1968). He was a pioneer in military aviation and a key figure in the creation of the RAF.

The Farmer: Jock Martin

Jock Martin was a good-looking man. His letters to Joan date from 1922 to 1923, when she was in her early twenties. How much Joan felt for him is in doubt, but to date he was the most hopeful suitor and they certainly enjoyed a dalliance of a kind. We know little about Jock, but he took Joan to the Hippodrome and to a cinema in Bristol one Saturday evening and they did not get home until nearly midnight, and then spent the next evening together. Jock reminded Joan: 'I think you enjoyed that night darling, I know I did, but not so much as the Sunday evening after . . .'

Jock then moved to Hockley House, Marton, near Rugby, where he was doing a stint as a farmer, helping a Mr Anderson; amongst his duties was the milking of two cows. He arrived there to find a letter from Joan, and told her: 'You are a little angel, darling, to be so thoughtful and waste all your time writing me letters but I do love getting them.' He declared that he felt 'quite jealous' that a friend had helped her with a broken mowing machine, and declared: 'I am longing, darling, for the time when I shall see you next.' Jock hoped to come to Windsor soon, but there was a problem: 'I expect I can come to you (si j'ai du *Cash*). Isn't it rotten father has docked me down to £2 a month and I get 10/- a week here so I'm £1 poorer a month. Swindle I call it.'

Jock addressed her as 'My dearest little girl' in March and 'My own dearest one' in June, which sounded rather warmer. Indeed by June he was declaring that he was 'simply aching to see you darling, more and more every day'.

For Joan's twenty-first birthday he sent her a watch, which pleased her. He was 'horribly jealous' that she had an escort to take her about, and he promised that when he came down to see her, she would 'lie down in the hammock' while he did all the work. The papers do not record Joan's reaction to what he proposed to serve, but it does not sound appetizing: 'My speciality in cooking is fried chips, onions and sardines. Mix them all up and add a little salt and it's A1.'

Jock revealed himself as more of a suitor in the letter he wrote in August, in which he suggested that had they gone to a garden party, 'we would have hopped off down to the hay loft or somewhere and enjoyed ourselves, what say you?' He then developed his theme, writing of how much he had enjoyed an evening with her in the billiard-room at home:

> Father is a cute 'Old Bird'. I think he knew perfectly well that we didn't do much dancing up in the billiard-room, dear. Anyway he's hinted as much, but on those sort of occasions he's *Blind*. Not so the noble Ma. How I laughed when one day she was saying she thought it very wrong for boys and girls to kiss unless they were engaged. Still darling no matter. We were quite happy, that was the main thing . . .

In October Jock sent Joan a little brooch. His last surviving letter came in February 1923, by which time he was still immensely amiable, but his ardour had cooled.

The Club Secretary: Neville De Rinzy

Joan had another friend, of whom she was fond for a long time: Neville L. C. De Rinzy. We know little of him, except that the De Rinzys were a very old Irish family who came originally from Clobemon, Co. Wexford, that he had a spinster aunt, Catherine, who lived in Dublin, and a sister who married an architect. He was another school friend of Reggie's at the Imperial Service College, and his career included serving in the First World War, being badly wounded, undertaking further service overseas, followed by the traditional and rather depressing settling-down of the unexceptional officer into civilian life. On a random check of the reference books he was still in England in 1939, but seems to have gone to live outside the British Isles thereafter.

Neville would probably resist the description of himself as 'Joan's boyfriend'. Nevertheless, she preserved his letters as of importance to her and I began my quest of him in that light. It is possible that I am a little hard on him, perhaps because the relationship did not develop. Neville came into Joan's orbit in the guise of her brother's friend. He was fond of Reggie's sister and in due course he graduated to become an object of hero worship and love. By well-established custom, when the sisters loved someone they did so with complete and total devotion, like trusting children. Neville remained in favour for twenty years, grateful for the dutiful letters Joan wrote him in his many overseas posts, grateful too that she remembered his birthday, for the gifts of handkerchiefs and hand-knitted socks. She was consistent in this loving devotion; he rather less so.

Was Neville in any way worthy of this devotion? He was not. He was a hearty man, limited in many ways, a good sort no doubt, uncomplicated by much thought or introspection, a man who lived from day to day, looking forward to his next sporting fixtures. Moustached, he had a rather unattractive mouth, giving the impression that he could be ungenerous or disapproving. He was probably not unlike many a young officer of his time, dutiful, straightforward, an asset to his regiment, but of no particular merit.

Neville appears less admirable to contemporary eyes than he would have done in his own time. His type has gone out of fashion with the passing of the years. The other question, more relevant to this story, is: did he make Joan happy in any way? Did he indeed set out to do so? The answer is that as far as she was concerned he proved a great disappointment.

Neville was born in October 1896, and, after Imperial Service College, he joined the 15th East Yorkshire Regiment, serving in France and Belgium. An early postcard records him 'off to the trenches for the 7th time of asking'. He was wounded in June 1915, and like Reggie, awarded the Military Cross. He spent some time in hospital at Le Trefont, before returning to 'dear old England'. The Red Cross Hospital for Officers in Park Street he dubbed 'a ripping hospital'. From his bed there he asked Joan to send his love to that other colleague, Harry Jacob, whose whereabouts he did not then know.

In August Neville continued his recuperation at Mrs Greville's Hospital at her home Polesden Lacey, later the house in which King George VI and Queen Elizabeth spent part of their honeymoon. Royalty were in evidence during Neville's stay: 'The King and Queen [George V and Queen Mary] came down to see us all today and shook hands with everybody and talked to us. He is awfully nice and very jolly, the Queen is very stiff and prim.'

Neville was consistent in all his communications to Joan in apologizing for letters left long unanswered, and in the wish to come and see her being frustrated by his other plans. As he recovered, he was 'flying all over the country staying with people'. Then he was sent off to Demerara, British Guiana, to oversee recruiting meetings at Police Headquarters in Georgetown. Back home in the latter months of 1917, we find him writing a letter of abject apology to Mrs Kappey for not having written before. Breezily he adds: 'I am quite certain I owe Joan a letter & I suppose she loves me no more now. I shall have to put on sack cloth & ashes!'

He proved too busy to see her before he sailed for India 'for goodness knows how long' in 1918, because he had been

'flying round saying goodbye & buying clothes & uniform'.
Again he added: 'There are several very great pals of mine
going so we ought to have a good time.'

The great thing about Neville's letters is that they were
always about himself. Also they were sufficiently few and far
between to give him a splendid excuse for a résumé of his
career of several recent months or even a year at a time. He
reached India in 1919 after a false start, and a 'topping voyage'
which he thoroughly enjoyed. By the summer of 1920 he was
on the North-West Frontier at Peshawar, after a lot of moving
about. He did not take part in any of the operations to quell
Indian riots, though he reported that 'things have been very
lively here on the Frontier and another Afghan war has only
just been averted'. He bought a horse and had 'some very
good fun with him', and presently took up polo in a big way.

Indian life became enviable in retrospect as Neville was
moved to Mesopotamia in December 1920, 'a different part of
the world, & certainly the worst I've ever been in'. They
marched 500 miles in three months: 'We didn't see much
scrapping but had one day's quite good fighting; we've been
very lucky & only had three casualties all in my company. We
finished up with a twelve days continuous march without a
rest starting about 8.30 every morning & finishing just before
dark.' Thus he arrived at Mosul 'deep in snow. It sounds
horrible.' It was to be his base for some time. Still, Neville was
ever optimistic: 'I'm looking forward to some rugger this
season.' Neville ran the regimental rugger team and was
proud of their prowess and record in the game.

Neville clearly took a dim view of the thinking man. Informing Joan that he was still in 'this abomminal [*sic*] country'
in April 1921, he continued: 'As the poets say: Spring has
come – and things are a bit brighter.' Rugger, polo and racing
were more his line, and with prolonged descriptions of these

he concluded, 'I think I've about exhausted all my news.' It must have seemed very strange when read out at Dargai in the bosom of the small impoverished family trying to make ends meet, and loyally keeping in touch with the soldier overseas.

In his particular way Neville was grateful for Joan's letters, but sensitivity was not his strong point. When she was twenty she sent him a snap of herself. To this he responded: 'Do you know Joan you look most awfully fat. I'm not meaning to be rude but it is such a long time since I saw you last & then you were much smaller. I'm sure I shouldn't recognize you . . .'

Soon after her twentieth birthday Joan attended the Henley Regatta and various dances at Sandhurst. This prompted Neville to report on his own enthusiasm for dancing:

I'm simply mad keen on dancing & did a tremendous amount in India. I danced with a girl, most of the time, all over the place, who was considered the best in India & who I know was considered the best in London a couple of years ago. The guest nights here when the Band plays all the latest things from town, it makes me itch to be at it again, but not much chance here except for an occasional hop given for the sisters at the Hospital, none of whom are much good. They are the only women in the place & only seven of them.

The boredom of Mosul was relieved by an unpleasant incident which Neville reported in September that year:

About a fortnight ago I was bathing in a backwater of the river with four or five of the other officers when one, the Adjutant, suddenly disappeared & we didn't see him again until I fetched the body out the next afternoon. It was a most awful shock to us all & a great loss to the Regiment. Since then no one has been very keen on bathing. Personally I haven't been in since.

And so it continued. By 1922 Neville was captain of his regimental hockey, rugger and cricket teams, and vice-captain of polo. He had added poker to his various recreations and was playing a spot of golf. He shot grouse, partridge and duck, having fun whenever possible. But reality crept in when he sent a message to Reggie, advising him to steer clear of Mesopotamia:

> He doesn't want to come anywhere near this cursed country. The hot weather has started to come in earnest now & is attended by the usual discomforts in the shape of mosquitoes, flies, bugs, & sickness. Small pox is pretty rampant in the town which is consequently 'out of bounds' & we've run 2 cases in the Regiment, neither of which luckily have proved fatal.

Neville hoped to get home after two years away, and only dreaded that the regiment might be sent to Ireland: 'We've had quite enough excitement & worry in the past two years without getting more on our return.'

In November Neville succeeded in getting a free passage on the *Braemar Castle*. His only sadness on leaving was that he would miss his polo ponies. He reached London, full of promises of a visit to Windsor, but the surviving correspondence contains endless apologies for not finding the time to make the journey; there are no letters of thanks following such a visit. He was always about to appear: 'I've got lots to tell you but will spout it all out when I see you. In awful haste Joan, old thing, my love to you all.' After that it was a septic leg, then Christmas, then Neville's skiing holiday in Switzerland. He was a busy man. The skiing was a success: 'I had a really topping time. I loved every minute of it & thoroughly enjoyed myself. I became quite good on skis before I left & am looking forward to next year.'

Presumably he did appear from time to time. Indeed one later letter refers to a visit, while apologizing for not making a further promised call. Throughout 1923 and 1924 it was the same story. In December 1924 Neville wrote: 'I had three weeks down in Aldershot in October & had hoped to have got over to see you but I couldn't get away, and had to rush back here [Lichfield] as soon as I could.' In 1925 he was still making excuses. In 1927 he was stationed at Abakaliki in southern Nigeria, and his later letters apologized for not replying sooner, thanking Joan for remembering his birthday: more socks and hankies. In 1929 he was promoted Major in the 2nd Nigeria Regiment. He used to send Christmas cards, and regrettably some of these would be considered unacceptably racist in a politically correct age. One such depicted two sparsely clad natives, the printed caption reading, 'Likely recruits'.

By November 1931 Neville had been married for over a year, yet Joan was still in touch and still remembering his birthday. In August 1934, at the age of thirty-seven, he became Secretary of the Sonning Golf Club. There he lived with his wife, Gwen, and two golden retrievers. After 1934 nearly twenty years of correspondence with Joan apparently ended. He was still at Sonning in 1939, but thereafter he disappears. What became of him is by no means as important to us as it would have been to him. He stands as an example of someone on whom Joan bestowed her affection, but who did not return it. Many others would have let him drop when the teenage crush wore off, but Joan was both tenacious and loyal, a good and loving friend.

Neville was of no use to Joan. Her devotion to him, nurtured in adolescence and sustained into adult life, fell on stony ground.

17

The Fiancé: Nigel

In my quest for further boyfriends, the next I found was Nigel, though he dates from a slightly later period. His letters were written between February 1936 and April 1937. I cannot be certain that there were not others in between, but he was the last important one, and indeed Joan's last chance of real happiness. This boyfriend went further than the others. He proposed marriage and was accepted.

Joan met Nigel (his surname still defies discovery) when she was staying with one of her maternal uncles, Stuart Mills,* at Cecil Road, Norwich. Nigel was a serviceman, attached to the North Suffolk Yeomanry Field Brigade, but then living on a yacht called *Lady Clare* at the nearby riverside town of Brundall, in Norfolk. He spent his time overhauling this vessel, indeed he was involved in extensive boat-building works, while simultaneously running a farm with pigs, ermines, rabbits and other livestock, tending a number of plants, and occasionally going to lectures or rushing off to take part in a parade or drill. His mother lived there too and he had one or two friends with whom he went sailing or took a drink in the evenings.

What else do we know of Nigel? He was not a self-confident man. He had once been engaged to a girl who later made a

* R. Stuart Mills (1876–1969).

name for herself on the stage and in films. She was called Enid Stamp-Taylor.* But the engagement had come to naught. Nigel smoked a pipe and he loved his car. He had no money. By his own admission he was poor at expressing himself, though he had his moments and his innate sincerity shone through every word he wrote. In his first letter, he told Joan: 'I can't begin to tell you on paper how much I worship you. It is absolutely beyond my poor powers. All I can say is – I love you darling more than anything else in the world.'

His second letter must have warmed her heart:

You remember I said in my last letter I loved you more than anything else in the world. Well, now you can just multiply that by ten million and then add another million, million. Then you might arrive at somewhere near a quarter the

---

* Enid Stamp-Taylor (1904–1946) was a popular comedy and character actress who had many leading parts in revues and musical comedies between the wars. She was born at Whitley Bay, Northumberland, and made her début in the chorus of *A–Z*, having won a beauty contest at the age of eighteen. She was soon given a leading part. She acted with Evelyn Laye in *The Belle of New York* at the Coliseum, and took part in many films, including *The Lambeth Walk* (1939), *Spring Meeting* (1941), *Hatter's Castle* (with Deborah Kerr and Robert Newton, 1941), and *The Wicked Lady* (with Margaret Lockwood and James Mason, 1945).

Enid married Sydney Colton in 1929, and had one daughter. The marriage was dissolved in 1936. In January 1946 she began to suffer cerebral haemorrhages, and as the result of one of these, fell in her bathroom and fractured her skull. She never regained consciousness and died four days later in hospital. She was forty-one.

There is a sad reference to Enid in Cecil Beaton's diaries. He visited Lady Cunard, who told him: 'Wasn't it *terrible* about that poor Miss Enid Stamp-Taylor! She slipped on a cake of soap in the bath, and the fall killed her!' (*The Years Between*, p. 215). I asked Nora Swinburne if she remembered her: 'Yes, I do remember Enid Stamp-Taylor; she was a beautiful woman with lovely skin. She and Jeanne Stuart, who is now baroness something, were of about the same period,' replied the 92-year-old.

correct answer. I am writing this in the cold grey light of dawn, with the rain pelting down, so I'm perfectly sane and in my right mind – dearest – I love every little bit of you, from the top of your sweet pretty head to the tips of your toes: you know I can't believe you love me too. It seems absolutely incredible and wonderful. It just beats me what you can see in such a perfectly ordinary bloke. You must have had hundreds of better chaps to choose from . . .

Nigel swore undying devotion. During February and March 1936 there were a number of intense meetings and all went well. But Nigel feared what might happen when Joan returned to Windsor after a stay on the boat, as she did towards the end of March. A few days later, although they were both suffering from rather unromantic colds, Nigel proposed marriage and was accepted. The discussion turned towards the question of a ring for Joan. 'You've made me feel I'm worth something,' wrote Nigel touchingly. 'And yet, quite often when I look into your eyes, I feel like a small speck of dust before the sun.'

Expressing himself with more confidence, Nigel wrote: 'The World is a good World. Life is no longer one dull day after another, but something vital, to be lived and enjoyed to the full. My darling, you never need have any fears of my being unfaithful to your trust: I couldn't be. After you, I'm afraid, other women rather disgust me; you are my life, my love, my all . . .' This went down badly, Joan complaining that she had never accused him of potential infidelity. Nigel apologized, calling himself a 'clumsy oik' and begging forgiveness for his 'clumsyness and oikishness'.

His message was unswerving: 'I am absolutely and completely yours for all time.' In late March, Joan went home, and when Nigel bade her farewell at the station he failed to kiss her and was in trouble again. This too he explained. He had not wanted to embarrass her in public. In Norfolk he continued his boat-building activities, with military commitments from time to time. Writing as soon as Joan left, he declared: 'Sweetheart, I'm just longing for the moment when I shall hold you close in my arms again. Joan, I want you so much. I would willingly give all I have just to have you back here again even for an evening.'

They were to be parted until 21 May. Joan sent him some trees which he planted with reverence. And she sent him a scarf which he wore proudly when shopping in Norwich. Soon afterwards she sent him some handsome driving gloves. In April, soon after Easter, Joan went to see her formidable Aunt Clare. This rather worried Nigel, who inquired nervously:

> How was Aunt Clare? And what did she think about you going and getting engaged – not so good – I bet. You know Joan you should have picked a gilded youth who could have given you a beautiful home and all sorts of lovely things, but eventually it was not to be. The ways of love are truly strange.

Joan reassured Nigel, as he confirmed: 'As you say, sweetheart, money isn't everything – no – not by a long chalk, and if we can just manage to scrape together enough to live on – well I personally ask for no better fate.' Joan was content, but Nigel was right to worry about Aunt Clare, whose concept of life and of how things should be arranged were rather different. Nevertheless, Clare issued an invitation to lunch during his stay in Windsor, which he was delighted to accept.

There was still time for a silly misunderstanding. Nigel drew some funny faces in his letter, one of which was captioned: 'Do yer still luv us?' Joan interpreted this as a warning that he might not love her and that he might break her heart. He put her mind at rest:

> You are all I've got. If I should lose you there would be nothing else to live for. It wouldn't matter to me if the wretched girl had twenty thousand a year, I'd see her in hell before I'd marry her. All I want is you. I have you, my sweet, and you only, for ever and always.

Nigel came down to Windsor on 21 May for the three days before he was due at camp at Currenden Farm in Swanage. The visit appears to have gone off well as Nigel wrote from camp that he loved her more than ever: 'My waking thoughts are always of you, even at night when I dream you are always there, Joan sweetheart. I shall always love, worship and adore you. Even as death's cold fingers twine themselves round my heart, my last thoughts will be of my great love for you.' Nigel went back to Windsor on 5 June for four more days with Joan.

Back in Norfolk, Nigel considered his future. He had applied for the Colonial Office, but was told he was too old except perhaps for an appointment in the West Indies. He tried for that, but in vain. They hated being parted, but Nigel was confident:

> We certainly are going to get married by hook or by crook, and that right soon. I just can't stand life any longer without you, it's no use trying. As you say if only we could get a start on our own. I know all would be well. It's just a matter of the first kick. If I could raise a capital of a thousand pounds, I could marry you just as soon as you were ready and I could safely say that within a year our income would be slightly over £250. Not too bad for a start.

Joan was very positive, replying that they could surely manage on £100. Nigel suggested that they should have a serious discussion in July and aim to marry the following June.

The summer progressed with a mixture of meetings and depressing separations. More gifts passed between Joan and Nigel. While his life went on much the same as ever in Norfolk, Joan got about Windsor, attending sherry parties and teas, both traditional forms of entertainment amongst the Kappeys and their friends. She went to see Aunt Clare, who was positioning herself as a negative force. In late July Nigel inquired anxiously, 'Hope you did your stuff well with Aunt Clare?' The question of Nigel's job arose again. The possibilities were that he might become a garage-hand in London, or join a company that made fans, run by one of Joan's cousins. (This job was squashed by Joan's mother because it was involved with the theatre, and Mrs Kappey disapproved.) Nigel did not mind really as long as he was near her.

Joan was due to pay a visit to the boat for a week beginning on 10 August, but this was delayed. Meanwhile rain fell in torrents. She finally arrived by train, armed with rubber boots, deck shoes and overalls. Following this visit, Nigel and his mother agreed that the best thing was to put the boat-building shed and all the farm stock at the disposal of her son, and also agreed to continue to contribute her share of house-keeping expenses. The yacht would be docked and sold in order to expand farming activities wherever they chose to settle. Nigel would put his hand to anything required to make a go of it. Then, assuming that Joan's mother approved, he and Joan would find a place together 'and move in bag and baggage and *get going*'.

To begin with, Joan's mother did approve. Nigel's mother was happy with any scheme that Joan's mother chose to make. But she was nervous at the prospect of meeting Mrs Kappey, feeling that she was of higher social station. Nigel reported:

She says although she would very much like to meet your mother she doesn't see her way clear at the moment to get away; she goes on to say that any mother of Joan's must be one of the best and that she approves *absolutely* and *completely* of you; your family; connections; and forebears: in fact that I am the luckiest of men and we have her blessing 'so get on with it' etc. For her part she begs to assure your mother that she is (my ma that is) respectable, no vices etc. etc. ad lib, and that as soon as she can possibly do it she will make it her business to call upon her; so as far as I can see all is well.

I told mother that your mother thought I was wild and consorted with a wild set – well she is still laughing. She says that considering the fact that she has known me all my life, she is in a position to say with the best authority that I'm not that sort, and never will be.

Nigel suggested they announce their engagement formally in the *Yorkshire Post* and the morning papers.

It was now September and Joan told Nigel she was feeling depressed. She did not explain why, but she did tell him that Aunt Clare had returned from her holiday in Baden-Baden feeling not too well. Nigel himself hated being parted from Joan and was pressing hard for a house-hunting expedition together. He was writing many letters for jobs, but to no avail. He came down again and spent more time with Joan, her mother and Aunt Clare.

By late September Nigel's problem had crystallized and while professing the undying love he held for Joan, he spilled out his woes:

I have been thinking terribly hard and though I hate to have to say so, I feel that we could under NO circumstances live all together in perfect peace and amity. Your mother, I fear, does not approve of me or my friends or of my outlook on life, in fact I fear I shall be totally unable to live up to her high ideals of what a pukka gentleman should be.

She possibly forgets that conditions of life have changed and are not the same as they were 40 or 50 years ago.

I admit I'm no tinpot saint on wheels, and I don't think you would like me to be, but that is apparently what is expected of me by your mother, and I repeat I can't live up to it, and I defy any man who is a man to do so under present-day conditions. As for running after all the women, and degrading myself by taking a subordinate position, the narrowness of the suburban outlook leaves me aghast. However the fact remains and will remain, I love, worship and adore you better than anything in the whole wide world.

Mrs Kappey, no doubt ably assisted by Aunt Clare, was doing her best to frustrate a romance that she judged unworthy of her daughter. Her problem was well identified by Nigel. All the early life with the Maharajahs in India and the regiment had caused her to uphold certain standards and beliefs. She was poor, but she was proud too. She still exerted a strong control on her daughter, though Joan was now thirty-six years old. She decided that Nigel was not good enough, and she let him see it, every day of his stay, including Sunday. According to him, she judged him a Victorian melodrama villain, who cared nothing for her daughter, who drank, consorted with evil companions, and chased every pretty face he saw. It is not the Nigel we know from his letters. Furthermore she humiliated him for his background. He was not, he admitted, 'a pukka Poona Sahib', but as he declared, 'I do, and I'm proud of it, come of a long line of County squires, and some of the finest blood of England runs in our veins.' Mrs Kappey did not believe him.

The strain began to weigh on Nigel, as he contemplated his

options: borrowing a cottage, where they could live together with his mother helping; selling the yacht – but the yacht might not sell; and finally getting a job. Like all lovers, he longed for a place alone, just the two of them:

> I know your mother would help us all she could in the way we have already discussed but so long as she continues to think of me as a sort of cross between Don Juan and Casanova, with a craving for drink, the plan becomes hopeless, as I know you will readily see. I am willing to do anything to have you my darling, but to try and live with a mother-in-law who has got the idea firmly fixed in her head that one is a drunkard, liar and general debauchee is absolutely out of the question . . .
>
> WE MUST ACT *NOW*. I'm not going to allow anyone or anything to come between us now; and woe betide anyone or anything that tries. You might pass that warning on. I should hate to do anything for which I should be sorry afterwards . . .

Joan began to think they had a 'hopeless outlook', but Nigel was not to be defeated. He had even found a cottage in Suffolk with a rent, until 1939, of £40, but he could not afford it. With a mere £200 Nigel reckoned they could make a start. Every now and again there were hints that Aunt Clare might help, but nothing ever came of this. Aunt Clare never got further than saying, 'If I did help . . .' She questioned whether Joan really thought that Nigel was prepared to marry her, which was all part of the general undermining process.

Poor Nigel tried to answer the further accusations levelled at him by Mrs Kappey:

> I am glad you think your mother is fond of me deep down. I fear it must be a long way down and very, very deep. But

what in Heaven's name makes her think I'm wild? and that theatrical people smashed my life? For a start I never knew any. When I was engaged to Enid Stamp-Taylor she had not gone on the stage; and did not for three years after.* I admit I have taken a chorus girl or so to supper, but that was many years ago; and everybody of my own age and class were doing likewise. All perfectly harmless and very callow; we all did it.

Now let me dispose of the drinking accusation.

You people who have lived all your lives in a small town in (forgive the expression) a terribly suburban atmosphere, cannot understand that in the country there are just two or perhaps three classes. 1. The gentry. 2. Farmers. 3. Labourers. Now the local Pig and Whistle is a club more than a pub. It is a meeting place where gentry, farmers and labourers meet on common ground, discuss stock crops and all the news of the day. More business is transacted in a country pub than anywhere else. It isn't like a town, where the lowest of the low congregate to get tight and have swearing matches. You must get that impression out of your head. When you have lived in the country for a little while you will understand what I mean better.

In the outside world, the autumn of 1936 was overshadowed by the growing crisis of the Abdication. Joan and Nigel were too preoccupied with their own problems to consider what was taking place. One joke slipped through in December, though: 'They are going to call the *Queen Mary*'s sister ship *Mrs Simpson*. Because she's faster but not so steady.'

The difficulty of separation grew on Nigel while Joan

---

* Enid Stamp-Taylor went on the stage soon after she was eighteen, so Nigel may have been economical with the truth here.

became accordingly pessimistic about the situation. Through October and the rest of the winter Nigel seemed able to bear up and held fast to his devotion. One after another, the job interviews proved hopeless. The situation was aggravated by Joan's jealousy of women and her mother's warnings about what she took for Nigel's weakness for any female. To avoid trouble, Nigel felt obliged to seek employment in all-male company:

> I can't think of one single job I could take on where women don't come into it somewhere, and as apparently I'm not to be trusted within a yard of a strange female I've practically given up hope. Why in God's name I should be so distrusted I don't know. Thousands and thousands of men spend their entire working life among women and yet they are happily married. I'm beginning to think I'm a sort of sex maniac or something. If this is so, I'd better go into a home for mental defectives at once.

Joan was torn between wanting to be with Nigel and her inbred need to stay at home and help her widowed mother. She made strenuous efforts to help him, but nothing seemed to work. Mrs Kappey and Aunt Clare offered some modest help eventually, and Nigel thought that if they could find a place, his mother would help too (with a pension of £180 a year). She would live with them at the start, and they should marry in the spring. Nigel listed the advantages and the disadvantages. The positive side was that they would marry, they would have some breeding stock and the benefit of £180 a year. The negative was that his mother would live with them for a year, it would be 'dashed hard work for all', he worried about the money, and there would be 'no pictures, no beer, no gadding about, no joy-rides in car, etc.' Nigel declared: 'I can stick it, but can you??'

Joan did not reply conclusively to this, but welcomed the wing of a lesser grebe, shot by Nigel, to be used as a hat ornament. The climate in Norfolk became bleak. Nigel's mother was unwell; in December there were high tides and floods, and Nigel and his mother were cut off from the world, communicating by flag signal or morse lamp. Conditions were grim. Then Nigel's uncle invited him and his mother to Yorkshire for Christmas, all expenses paid, but Joan suddenly announced she was coming up and so he cancelled.

Joan arrived, but we do not know how the Christmas visit was. However, by 8 January 1937 she and Christian were staying with their uncle Stuart in Norwich, and Nigel was not sounding as ardent as hitherto. Though he continued to send all his love, life had become even more of a strain. He fell ill, the gas failed, he often cancelled Joan's visits. Joan remained in Norwich until April. Meanwhile Nigel applied for the RAF and went for a test. 'I don't think I'll pass,' he wrote. 'Anyway, if I don't, it will only be just one more disappointment – life to me seems to be made up of them. Anyway you can rely on me to do my very best. But for God's sake don't expect anything.'

There were the usual meetings and then in April there came a serious crisis in their relationship. What probably happened is that Nigel gave up, unable to cope any more. He had been worn down by the attempts to get a new life going, the numerous failed job interviews and the onslaughts on his character from Joan's mother. Nigel let Joan know that for a time it was better that they act like brother and sister.

Mrs Kappey fell into an Edwardian decline at the news, devastated at the way her daughter had been let down. She had of course effectively destroyed Joan's last chance of real happiness, so she had cause to be guilty. Joan could not believe that the end had come and even suggested that Nigel might have found another woman. On 8 April he responded:

Now let's get this other woman question straightened out. This applies to all of 'em. I'm fed up to the teeth with all of them, their actions, ways and outlook on life, and what's more the least I have to do with them the better I shall be pleased. So you needn't worry about my doing any love making, because it just won't happen.

I do care for you, Joan, and always will, but I am going to live the life of a monk for a while and get on with my job, without feminine interference of any sort.

I don't see what your mother has to be unwell for, as that you and I should break it off was her dearest wish; she was always ramming it down my throat and now that we've done, even for a little while perhaps, she pretends to be cut up about it – tripe and onions!

If it's hit her so badly what the devil did she mean by always going at you to break it off for?? . . .

I am still trying for the RAF and hope to know something definite within the next week or two, as the sooner I get away from Norfolk the better I shall be pleased. I want to start a new life with a clean sheet, and just see what I can do if I try. You never know I might be a man of millions within the next six months!

I must stop now and get on with my work. Meanwhile Joan, for Goodness' sake snap out of it and try and look forward to a bright future . . . Write and let me know when you have got back safely as I still think of you lots!! God bless you and keep you.

A week later Nigel politely declined the idea of a meeting: 'I should love to – BUT – I don't think that any useful purpose would be served, so I really think we'd better not.' Incredibly, Nigel had now got a job working in a neighbouring boatyard, and would soon be going to sea for a while. Towards the end

of April, Nigel wrote Joan his last letter, from the motor yacht
Gay Venturer, then in Southminster, Essex:

> You see that I have started my career as a seafaring gentle-
> man well. I am in command of the above 200 ton yacht,
> belonging to a London City Magnate, and incidentally
> drawing damn good pay. I have a crew of 12 under me, and
> you can bet I make 'em work. We shall only be here for
> another week to finish fitting out, then ho for London River
> for the Coronation.* Then Cowes, then Ostend, and cruise
> down the French coast to the Riviera to finish the season;
> this is a *permanent* all the year round job, so I'm well away!!
>
> Cheerio old thing.

---

* The Coronation of King George VI and Queen Elizabeth took place on
12 May 1937.

18

Christian's Holiday

Life went on at Dargai in Clarence Road, and despite Joan's occasional attempts to escape with various boyfriends, it was to that home that she always returned. She submitted once more to the domination of her mother and to that strange world where the dead held sway with almost equal power as the living. Until the end of her life Mrs Kappey maintained the charade that her long-dead husband was still alive, just as Violet Jacob had for some years sent Joan and Christian presents in the joint names of herself and her dead son. All this Joan accepted as par for the course, though at times it may have weighed heavily on her and caused her to be introverted.

Christian was a more outgoing person, less intense, a little more frivolous, loving a party or an expedition, and thoroughly good-natured. Sometimes it would seem she enjoyed herself a little too much, returning home from the inevitable sherry party a little 'squiffy'. Joan and her mother were not altogether approving.

In one of the letters to Joan from Jock Martin in March 1922, he alludes to a holiday taken by Christian: 'So Chris has been away. I wonder whether she met any nice people.'

Christian's best break was in 1925 when she went down to Devon towards the end of the year as a guest of her cousin Cecil. Chris saw a schoolfriend off to Paris, and ten friends then went to a show. There were visits to Badminton, a series of rugger matches to watch and numerous dances. Christian sent home postcards of dogs every day. Unfortunately Queen Alexandra died during her stay and several dances were cancelled out of respect.

Despite that, Chris's sense of fun was undimmed as she related her news to her mother:

> How too perfectly sweet of you to send me that dinky little evening dress, you are a *darling*. I thank you a thousand times. I was getting rather worried about one, as we have 5 or 6 dances coming off, & my taffeta is defunct, also Audrey's pink dress is rotting all over, so only had Oty's pale blue, as the beaded one isn't smart enough for a dance, they all wear very wonderful dresses.
>
> It has just come in time for Sat. week as we are going to the Royal with the Mac's again, & Jack Chalice is coming as my partner, is v. tall & a pet, is the best dancer in the battalion, they are all dining with us first. He came to tea yesterday, came back with us after the rugger match which we had watched. Cecil was playing for the Devonport Services v. the Army. The latter won. Honey came after tea (he was playing too) & supped with us & then took me to the theatre to see 'White Cargo',* which is 'Red 'ot'!! as Cecil says – a native girl, naked except for a loin cloth, tries to seduce a man. It is very well acted, & she is the only woman in the play . . .
>
> Don't know how you managed, you are darlings, not to have wired for me. I really am having a glorious time & should love to come back engaged, but don't expect I shall. B. & C. are doing their best!! & are priceless! . . .
>
> Bar & Cecil want me v. much to stay for Xmas but I've

* A play by Leon Gordon. It opened at the Playhouse in May 1924.

said I can't, but how long can you manage without me, as they want me to stay as long as poss! . . .

The answer was that Christian was needed at home, so she was duly reined back, returning without a ring on her finger.

19

Aunt Clare in Later Life

It is the privilege of the novelist to play havoc with time, and it is equally possible with this story to skip rather quickly over the intervening years until we move into the 1960s once more. The pattern was set, and it did not greatly alter. Life went on relentlessly at Dargai, with Mrs Kappey presiding over the household, her two daughters well controlled and at her side.

It is necessary to dispose of Aunt Clare and Mrs Kappey, and to reintroduce Major Clough and set the scene for the arrival of Dick Bonham.

Aunt Clare remained active despite her many griefs. She translated the memoirs of Princess Racowitza, and wrote articles for the *Ladies' Field*, using on both occasions the name of 'Cecil Mar'. It was quite usual at that time for grand ladies who wished to publish stories to do so under a pseudonym. According to the *Dictionary of National Biography*, Princess Louise, Duchess of Argyll, Queen Victoria's daughter, wrote magazine articles under the name of 'Myra Fontenoy', though none of her later biographers have been able to find them. Such a precedent would have been more than enough for Clare.

Clare published her memoirs anonymously in 1920. She was soon exposed, however. It was the *Ladies' Field* that broke the news on 24 July: 'The authorship of *From an Eastern Embassy*, recently published by Herbert Jenkins, Limited, has been divulged,' they wrote.

It is possible to get an idea of Clare's later life from a handful of postcards that survived in the house. She gave herself the most sybaritic life possible, treating herself by no means badly, summering and wintering abroad. July 1925, for example, found her wandering about the Alps, near the Château de Chillon, by Montreux. At some point before 1920 she remarried, to a man called George Ravenscroft, by his own description 'a gentleman', and they lived at 76 Carlton Hill, St John's Wood. At Christmas 1930 they were at Wiesbaden (a regular haunt), before moving in the new year to Monte Carlo, and thence to the Hotel Windsor at Cannes, where they stayed until March.

George Ravenscroft died at his home in St John's Wood on 4 March 1930 and his ashes were placed quietly and without fuss in the Brompton Cemetery. George left Clare with over £11,000. Clare suffered again, but she did not retreat from the world. In the early 1930s, she spent a Christmas at the Estorio Palacio hotel in Estoril, travelling by boat – 'first class food & attendance on board' – and settling into 'a most comfortable hotel, with plenty of people round one, friends here & as much gaiety as I can stand'. Clare enjoyed the sun and the proximity of the Atlantic and welcomed the fact that the Casino was in the grounds of the hotel. She was being cared for by a nurse and was 'up & down in health', she told her niece Joan in a letter. She pointed out that she liked to be known by her French title when abroad: 'Comtesse des Boullets Ravenscroft', as she put it.

Having given this far from unenviable description of her winter break to a family but one step above penury, she continued: 'I enclose a little cheque (10/- for each of you) to get a little Xmas gift from your old Aunt! I wish I could send more, but have very heavy expenses now.'

Clare's influence on her nieces remained strong. As we have

seen, her approval was sought when Joan wanted to marry Nigel, and at one time it seemed that Clare might help them rent a cottage, but ultimately no such help was forthcoming. Like Lily Kappey, Clare maintained the prejudices of an earlier age, particularly regarding class.

On 14 July 1933 Clare remarried for the third and last time. By now she was a rather handsome old lady with a long, royal nose, wearing a coat with feathers at the neck and a fur wrap cast round her shoulders. Some readers will know what I mean when I say she looked like a cross between Princess Marie Louise and Lady Ottoline Morrell.

Clare emerged from the Brompton Oratory as the second wife of a 76-year-old widower called Augustus Hughes-Hughes, formerly Assistant Keeper of Manuscripts at the British Museum. Gus clearly had a taste for the exotic mid-European. His first wife had been the stepdaughter of the Chamberlain to the King of Hungary. He looked the part too, with white hair, noble forehead and a more than handsome, well-groomed white moustache.

It would seem that Gus and Clare were happy together. Gus's granddaughter, young at the time, only had a vague memory of Clare as a not very agreeable figure, with exaggeratedly dyed red hair. It is a picture that fits. In August 1936 Gus and Clare summered for the first time at Bremer's Hotel, Baden-Baden, staying in splendid rooms. They loved the town and decided they preferred it to Wiesbaden. The following spring Gus fell seriously ill, returning to their home in Albert Hall Mansions with a nurse on 18 April.

Gus died on 2 January 1942, aged eighty-four, and Clare survived until 27 July 1944, dying in a cottage at Bray at the same age. In a macabre note in her will, she directed her executors 'to arrange for the operation of venesection to be performed upon my body in order to insure that life is extinct'. She was interred in her son's grave in Brompton Cemetery.

In a will made early in 1944, and with a codicil dated three days before her death, Clare left money to all her nieces (£500 each to Joan and Christian) but in effect more than that. (Clare left £11,743. 11s. in her estate.) She also bequeathed to Joan her larger diamond brooch, her half-hoop diamond ring, the larger silver-framed mirror, a silver-plated tea service and other items including her Chefakat decoration.

For years afterwards the Kappeys placed a memorial notice in the *Daily Telegraph*, 'in devoted memory of beloved Aunt Clare'.

20

Life at Dargai

From her earliest childhood, Christian loved to paint. Her parents could not afford to give her formal training, so she treated it as a lifelong hobby, enjoying her first exhibition at Ascot in 1973. She often painted flowers, many of which were to be found in her garden at Clarence Road.

During the war, Christian became a scene-painter at the Theatre Royal, Windsor, a job that she enjoyed enormously. They worked seven days a week. In one of those inspired morale-boosting decisions, the theatre had remained open throughout the war, and every Monday night the curtain rose on a new production. This required a great deal of work by all concerned, and the work was done by a happy team of seven men and two girls. By the time the director, John Counsell, returned from war, the Theatre Royal was a thriving concern. Chris wanted to make a career of this and could have done so, but her mother forbade it. Six years after the war, when she left, she did so with the best wishes of the Counsells, and a farewell gift signed by Russell Thorndike and others. She made one rather exciting friend as a result when her friend Ann married William Mervyn, who became a well-known actor. I remember him particularly for his part as the Bishop in *All Gas and Gaiters*. Chris used to lunch with them at Wraysbury.

Always more gregarious than her sister, Chris also took to

making pottery and was successful at this. Later too, she used to get wood-carvings sent over from Kenya by her brother, and sold these for a modest profit. She collected hundreds of glass objects.

In 1951 the two sisters were able to buy the freehold of Dargai for the sum of £850, and this secured the home that had been rented to them for so long. Mrs Kappey continued to preside over their lives, and in 1952 she sent Joan one of her traditional birthday greetings, as though the girls' father were still alive: 'Happy Birthday, Joan darling – With fond love from Daddy & Moosie, hoping it will always have a silver lining!'

The sisters still managed to get away from time to time, but their mother never relented in her demands. They themselves believed they adored her, and yet from her letters to them she emerges as a harridan, rebuking, cajoling and playing wounded, alternating this with assurances of her devotion to them. In 1954 Christian went to Glasgow to stay with an aunt. Mrs Kappey wrote: 'So glad to know you arrived safely when Joan rang up, but how tired you must have been after that long wait. After all you might have caught a later train! & given us time to finish our lunch in peace! . . . This morn Joan was splendid! up in time & brought my breakfast & managed well . . .' Another time Mrs Kappey forwarded a letter with the note: 'Sincerely hope it is not to say you have been over-drawing at the Bank!!'

Joan fared badly as she moved into middle age. June 1952 found her in the David Moore Ward of Holloway Sanatorium at Virginia Water, and in August 1955 she was in the same hospital once again. On the first occasion she went in for a rest, and her aunt Muriel wrote to her, 'I expect you have been doing *too much*. If you keep *smiling* & try & be brave dear I feel quite sure you will be yourself again before you realize it.'

Joan's second incarceration in Holloway came about in the

most sinister manner. She received a chain letter exhorting her to send it on and threatening bad happenings if she did not. She tore it up and almost immediately afterwards her dog, Tinker, died. Joan could not help believing that it was her fault and got into a state about it. Her doctor was away, another one came, and was frightened by her condition. Before Joan knew it she was back in Holloway and had been certified insane. She was put into a huge ward opposite the padded cells.

Christian appealed for help to a kind friend and neighbour, Charles Keeler, who went to see Joan and found her protesting: 'They're all mad here!' Mr Keeler was able to help Joan and succeeded in convincing the authorities that they should release her. After a little spell at Ridgemead House, a nursing home in Englefield Green, she was once again a free woman.

The days and months and years of life at Dargai must have seemed long and depressing at times, and as the sisters grew older there would have been no shortage of opportunity to become low in spirits. I am haunted by the remark made by a cousin at the gathering after Joan's funeral in 1987, which silenced the room and left everyone there rather subdued. 'Of course,' said the cousin, 'it was awful when one of the sisters tried to hang herself.' No one asked more about this, and I too have let it pass.

Mrs Kappey remained surprisingly strong, but in February 1957 she had to submit to the surgeon's knife. Relations with her son, Reggie, had not been close for some years. He wrote to her from his home in Kenya:

If your hemaroids [*sic*] are external it is simple. If internal the operation is nothing, but afterwards it is quite a bit painful doing your duty, but it must be done otherwise it will undermine your health . . . If your heart is sound there is nothing to fear & you will be good for many years. Now if God wills you pass on I will look after the girls so don't worry about that either, but I am sure that won't happen for some time. Keep your pecker up & DON'T be frightened . . .

Whether these words cheered Mrs Kappey we do not know.

Sometimes it was Joan who went away. She too received her share of missives, from Mrs Kappey. In 1957 Joan stayed with another aunt, Jeanie East, in Sussex. Mrs Kappey, then aged eighty-six, wrote to her 51-year-old daughter:

You don't seem to have taken many clothes with you dear, & I am wondering if you have been able to pick up a better hat to match that coat? . . . I don't feel too well. It has turned colder & still have beastly pain in back! Expect it is rheumatism & will see Dr about it when you return dear. Chris went to Major & Mrs Mills's sherry party last evening & quite enjoyed it! Didn't like the idea of going without *you* dear but I hired Mr Tilbey to take her there & back & many people there she knew & was quite jolly & didn't return home till 8.15 but quite sober!! Molly came in to be with me!! so was not left alone. She wore her green velvet dress & looked very pretty & everyone admired her! Most others wore *black*!

Another letter at about this time took up Mrs Kappey's old theme of the mother and one daughter struggling valiantly on while the other went out to play:

Chris has been splendid to keep the 'Home fires burning' so long without you, dear, & looking after your old Mother . . . Your *path* is groaning for your help! weeds all over as I have not felt like doing too much. Chris has tried to cut grass & Billy [Major Clough] came once to do it as with this humid weather it has grown apace, & leaves now falling from trees!! So don't get a shock dear after Auntie's trim one. We shall

try to have the house looking tidy for your return darling &
are excited at the thought of seeing you again . . .

By April 1960, Major Clough had become established as a
regular visitor and help to Chris and her mother. The gallant
old soldier could often be seen working away with watering-
can in hand, tie in place, but jacket off and waistcoat undone.
He had been a widower for two years, his wife of fifty-four
years having died in the Edward VII Hospital on 4 June 1958
at the age of eighty-one.

Christian's devotion to him went back at least as far as 1953;
it was possibly more than simple devotion, as a poem in Christian's hand, called 'To My Billy – Anticipation', suggests:

> The promise of the rising sun
> Your heart beats next to mine
> Knowing that our love is one
> And lingering, inter-twine
>
> The rapture of your closeness
> Of your soft and silky skin
> Pressed tightly to my body
> As you gently merge within
>
> Oh, wondrous glowing love
> Deepening as the depth of time
> Evolves the rocks from Heaven above
> We are one my Darling, you are mine.

I understood that Billy did not marry Christian because
he had promised his wife that he would always remain her
widower. June Bourne-May recalled Grace Clough saying:
'When I go, don't let that little Kappey get Billy!' It would
seem even more complicated, however, as at one point he
intended to leave some money to the good-looking widow of

another Military Knight, a lady rather younger than the normal line of such widows. We cannot know, but his friendship with Christian, so important to her, caused her a certain amount of anguish.

Whenever possible, Chris and Major Billy would go up to London, take lunch at the Naval and Military Club, and then scour London for soldier prints for his collection. They would return to his home in Windsor Castle for tea. Some of the Military Knights, and in particular his beady-eyed neighbour, Miss Gwladys Hanbury-Williams, a former Mayor of Windsor, viewed the friendship with a certain amount of disapproval.* There was a naughty streak in his character. The wife of one Military Knight recalled: 'He'd pinch your bottom for fourpence.' Then there was an afternoon when a visitor called and found the Major in jaunty mood, with Christian sitting on his knee. The Lower Ward hummed with the story.

In April 1960, when Joan was away and Billy was busy putting in potatoes, a Windsor neighbour, Denys Graves, was due to visit. At this point Dick Bonham makes his first appearance in the story. He came to tea with Mrs Kappey and Christian, brought by Francie Kavanagh, and 'stayed on for supper!! & didn't go till 10 o'clock', as Christian informed her sister.

On 18 January 1961, Mrs Kappey celebrated her ninetieth birthday. Reggie excelled himself as usual. An air-mail letter arrived late from him in Kenya. 'Just remembered it was your birthday yesterday,' he wrote. Mrs Kappey was now an eccentric old lady with long white hair, and in the summer she would sit in the garden in her dressing-gown, with bedroom slippers on or barefoot, protecting herself from the sun with a

* I recall meeting Miss Hanbury-Williams on the doorstep when I visited Major Clough in 1969. She almost spat her distaste for the *ménage*.

striped umbrella. Reggie's last letter to his ninety-year-old mother was sent to her a few days before she died, and was full of lame intent: '. . . hope that sometime next year we may take a trip home if we can afford it . . .'

July 1961 found Chris away in Sussex for four days, after an exciting visit to London where she had been joined by Major Clough. Her cousin Stella, with whom she was staying, judged her something of a country bumpkin and loaned her a 'v. snappy pr. of her sandals' which gave her confidence before they all went out to 'a very poche [*sic*] place in St James's' for dinner. Christian was beginning to free herself a little from the tyranny of the mother whom she adored, despite everything. She wrote to Mrs Kappey and Joan:

> It looks as if it is going to be very hot again today, so I do hope you will both take it easy, & remember that life is more important than the —— house & garden . . .

Mrs Kappey wrote a rather rambling reply, often repetitive, but affectionate: 'God bless & watch over you & bring you back to your old Mother safely, darling, & Joan's writing & is looking forward to your return . . .' Chris kept the letter in a special envelope marked 'Last letter from my darling little mother 1961'. Just two weeks later, on Sunday 16 July 1961, Mrs Kappey died in her room. The Kappey sisters were not unaware of the significance of this date: it was exactly forty-five years to the day since Harry Jacob had died for his country.

Betty Worthington recalled Christian's description of her mother's death: 'Poor little Chris said: "As mother died, she was upstairs, and I looked out and I saw her spirit come down the stairs . . ."'

From that day on, the two sisters were left to cope on their own.

Part Three

21

Joan's Knight in Shining Armour

Dick Bonham was the most unlikely man to be the object of an obsession. He was a bachelor who had failed to find his way in life. He was born at Colbinstown, Co. Kildare, on 1 May 1916, and had served in North Africa as a Lieutenant in the RASC. By profession he was a landscape gardener, tackling everything from windowboxes to large gardens. He had lived in Ireland, keeping bees and running a garden centre in Co. Meath. Later he lived in Somerset, Kew and Richmond before finally settling at The Links in 1954. The main reason he was there was because his powerful mother made it her home for some periods each year. But he was also a great favourite of Francie Kavanagh's and she needed a younger man about the premises. Another younger man in residence was Giles Howard, who was a great friend of his. Dick had a room at the top of the house.

Dick was as much Miss Kavanagh's right-hand man at The Links as Louis Murphy. Some have suggested that if anyone in the house could be deemed to be Francie's 'boyfriend', it was more likely to be Dick than Louis Murphy, despite the difference in age. But he seemed wholly uninterested in romantic attachments of any kind.

In the mid-1950s Dick suffered a nervous breakdown and endured a spell in Holloway Sanatorium. He underwent the unpleasant experience of electric shock treatment and he eventually got better. He remained subject to occasional depression, brought on by worry. He had very little security in life.

In 1957 Francie introduced Dick to Patrick O'Grady, who had married Mairi Macnab, the daughter of great friends of hers in Windsor. O'Grady had just set up a gardening business and Dick joined him as partner. They were good friends for the next quarter of a century. Mairi O'Grady recalled Dick looking like 'Ptolemy tortoise with his crumpled beige trousers and rounded back, often covered in a sheepskin jacket'. Dick was a keen gardener, though something of a flounderer. He was a great starter of projects which Patrick O'Grady was often obliged to tidy up or finish. At times Dick also worked with the distinguished garden designer, James Russell, of Sunningdale Nursery (who died in 1996).

While researching this book many years later I called on Dick's brother in Ireland. He recalled that Dick had many friends and a good sense of humour: 'He could even make his brother laugh!' he said. When I told his brother that Dick was to be a central character in my book, he said he thought the idea of being in a book might rather have appealed to Dick. 'Something to dine out on!' was his generous comment.

Dick was the scion of two rather grand extended families in Ireland, the Bonhams and the Hamiltons. The Bonhams were found in Dublin as early as 1712, and their estate was Ballintaggart, Colbinstown, Co. Kildare. They also had land in Wicklow and other places. Dick's grandfather had served at the Siege of Lucknow, and his father, Major John Bonham, was an estate agent who had gone out to the diamond mines of South Africa as a young man, and joined the Rhodesian Horse at the outbreak of the Second Matabele War. He lost an eye, and found the rigours of South African life injurious to his health. He came home and settled in Worcestershire, where he was a horse-breeder for fifteen years and rode with the North Cotswold Hounds. In the First World War he served with the Remount Service at Dunkirk and later at Cologne.

The Major married Lilian Hamilton,* of Hamwood, Dunboyne, Co. Meath, in 1911. The wedding was celebrated at St Peter's, Dunboyne, where the villagers put up triumphal arches over the road, bearing mottoes: 'God Bless the Happy Couple' and 'Health and Happiness to You Both'. Schoolchildren strewed roses before their feet.

The Hamiltons of Hamwood were another distinguished Irish family, spread widely across the Emerald Isle. In a family of ten, Lilian (or Lily) was the youngest of the six sisters, of whom two were distinguished artists whose works fetch good prices in the auction houses today. Eva was the eldest, a well-known portrait painter who had studied under Sir William Orpen. She had painted Lady Gregory and Oliver Fry, and had made a copy of 'The Lord's Supper' in Trinity College Chapel. Letitia Marion (May) was next, and certainly the best-known today, a painter of landscapes in Ireland and in Venice and Portugal, who studied under J. B. Yeats as a young girl. She was described as 'an outstanding and singular personality . . . at once a lady of quality and a painter of brilliance'. Amy, the third sister, was a social worker, and county secretary of the Women's Institute in Yorkshire; she travelled extensively. She returned to live in Ireland in 1946. Ethel, the fourth sister, suffered from rheumatoid arthritis and was confined to a bath-chair. She died in 1924. There was another sister, Constance, a landscape gardener. Of the six, only Lilian married.

Their father, a horticulturist and arboriculturist, was land

* She was the Mrs Bonham I met at lunch with Joan in 1969.

agent to the Duke of Leinster. The family was raised at Hamwood, a Palladian house near Dublin, built in 1764. How they
were all housed there is one of those Irish mysteries. One
brother, Freddie,* slept in the bathroom with the airing cupboard, 'to warm him up for India' in the words of Mrs
Charles Hamilton, who now lives at Hamwood. Anne Hamilton told Olda Fitzgerald: 'May was in love with George
Brooke† but of course wasn't allowed to marry him as he was a
first cousin, and Eva painted a picture of her sitting at a
window with an anxious expression, called "Will He Come?"'
Olda Fitzgerald described Hamwood in *Harper's & Queen* in
1988:

> In the overgrown walled garden there are arches for roses to
> climb up, and a little house in one corner where roses grow
> up the pink brick walls. The dappled undergrowth is sweet-
> scented after the rain. The leggy beech and spreading mag-
> nolia overshadow the hips and haws, maples grow into the
> bushy yews, and urns stand on the garden wall. 'There are a
> lot of redundant chimneys about the place,' sighs Charles
> Hamilton, looking at the laundry chimney and another
> which once heated the glass-houses. He eyes the autumnal
> wilderness with a regretful pleasure. 'I was going to put a
> digger through it, but then I thought, "Ah, I'll leave it stand
> a bit longer."'

During the war the surviving Hamilton sisters lived at Dun-
sinea House, Castleknock, and took in paying guests in much

---

* Lt.-Col. Frederick Hamilton, OBE, DL, JP, of the 8th Bengal Lancers
(1880–1962).

† George Brooke (1877–1914). Lieutenant, Irish Guards. In 1907 he married
Nina, daughter of Rt. Hon. Lord Arthur Hill. He was killed in action on the
Aisne.

the same way as Frances Kavanagh did at The Links. One lodger was a Prince Ghika, and in 1941 John Betjeman and his wife were their paying guests for six months while the poet was employed as Press Attaché to the British Ambassador, Sir John Maffey.

Betjeman soon learned that, besides Lily, the other sisters had been forbidden to marry by their father. They were poor and wore their fur coats indoors to stave off the cold. Their artistic and landed-gentry friends provided him with any number of connections. He described them as having 'kind hearts and loud voices' and declared that they gave him 'nervous attacks at breakfast every morning'. He thought the house 'very expensive – *very* cold' and noted that there was hot bath water only once a week. He observed that Connie Hamilton was in bed with frostbite 'contracted *inside* the house'.

After the war, the sisters moved to Woodville, having it in exchange for paying the rates of £70 a year, fixed for twenty years. This they outlived, though they were able to stay on. They lived there together, looked after by two old caretakers. Woodville was a rambling, dilapidated old house on the banks of the Liffey, and had stood empty for about forty years. It consisted of a central eighteenth-century block and a large late-Georgian wing. A feature of the house was a series of reception rooms along the garden front, with a bow-fronted drawing-room decorated with nineteenth-century white and gold wallpaper.

The four sisters took in further paying guests and these ranged from Trinity College students to a retired Group-Captain. By the late 1950s the old ladies were somewhat tweedy, but the house was still active and as Mark Bence-Jones recalled, 'During one [Dublin] Horse Show week, somebody dropped in and found Princess Maria Pia of Italy standing gracefully among the dogs' plates on the doorstep.' The sisters lived on into the 1960s. Amy died in February 1960, and her sister Eva a month later. The other two survived until 1964. Connie would be out in the garden and anyone who strayed across her would be treated to an impromptu horticultural lecture. May went on painting until within a week of her death, despite a tremor in her hand, and as one friend put it, 'She was having the time of her life.' May died in August 1964, and Connie in December that year, so they and Mrs Bonham survived during the early years of Joan's obsession with Dick.*

The sisters were a part of that 'doomed aristocracy' so typical of Southern Ireland this century, game old characters living in grotesque discomfort, surrounded by the vestiges of faded glory. They wore terrible old clothes, and had rugged old faces. They were delightfully eccentric and entirely true to their roots and upbringing. They knew how to have fun. This was the world in which Dick Bonham had grown up.

Joan met Dick Bonham soon after he arrived at The Links in 1954, but her obsession for him did not form until somewhat later on. By the middle of 1960 it was well rooted in her mind, and from her diary there is a strong implication that others had to fall from favour before Dick became the focus of her attention.

There is evidence of an obsession with a man called Jimmy Hill, whose name was linked with Joan's on a piece of blotting-paper which I found in the house, and for whom she prayed until February 1961. He was a naval commander, who lived at Arlington Lodge in Eastbourne. Joan telephoned him with great regularity in the late 1950s. This I know because at

* Mrs Bonham left Woodville in the mid-1960s, and some time later the house was demolished.

Dargai both sisters listed their calls on a piece of paper which, like the blotting-paper, survived and was still in the house when they died. The duration of each call was noted in order that each could pay her share of the telephone bill. But I know nothing more about Jimmy Hill and presumably he fell by the wayside when Dick appeared.

There is only one other protagonist in the story who needs to be introduced. He was a friend of Christian's called Denys Graves.

22

The Man with the Matinée Idol Looks

The Kappey papers on which I have relied so heavily for my information consisted largely of letters and notes. But there was also a vast collection of photographs. It was not unusual for a family like that to keep portraits of their friends and relations. But both sisters were themselves great recorders of their lives, and, if not necessarily inspired portraitists, they could both hold the camera steady and produce more than competent results. This was perhaps one of their greatest hobbies, and there survive a number of albums with photographs dating back to their days in India and continuing right into the 1970s.

In their later years Joan and Christian used to steer their guests out into the garden. There they would pose them always in the same spot – up against the garden wall. I found most of the characters in this story photographed in this way: Mrs Kappey, Major Clough, Lady Dorothy Palmer, brother Reggie and even, to my surprise, myself, caught as a long-haired youngster in 1971.

Obviously, the collection of Kappey photographs that survived at their house was largely formal. There were to be found an abundance of ladies in fine dresses, the occasional academic, a clergyman or two and a considerable number of soldiers. Equally, there was one face that recurred often that did not fit the pattern: the photograph of a matinée idol. This man was good-looking in a way, with sinister, rather polished good looks. He favoured a black shirt and a beige tie that matched his beige jacket. He was called Denys Graves.

For a long time I wondered how he fitted into the story. Was he possibly some kind of star of stage and screen? Was Christian a fan of his? Certainly he had presented her with a number of signed photographs of himself and these appeared to be publicity shots.

This collection of Denys photographs, kept by Chris, implied that he had aspirations to go on the stage or possibly wished to be a male model. His wavy hair was parted slightly left of centre and Brylcreemed into place. I cannot explain why, but looking at his photograph, I thought he looked untrustworthy.

There were also photographs of Denys with Christian. He was her friend. As such, of course, he risked being less liked by Joan, who suffered from jealousy. This proved to be the case. He had known Mrs Kappey too. In March 1960, about a year before she died, Mrs Kappey planned a tea-party and Denys Graves was on the guest list. On a page in Joan's diary which records this, there appears the first reference to '*Dick*' – later changed to 'My *Dick*'.

It took me a long time to find out who Denys Graves was. For ages he remained a mystery figure. At the beginning I knew more what he was not than what he was. He did not become a successful actor, nor was he one of the actors in the repertory company of the Theatre Royal, Windsor. Yet he must at least have attempted some career in the public eye. Later he lived at Kynance Place in London for a time, and after that in Petersham, Surrey.

At one time Denys sent a photograph of himself on the *Queen Elizabeth* with a largish lady. This he captioned 'Mary and I descending down to dinner!'. In 1963 he sent another photograph of himself on a beach in Biarritz. By this time his hair had thinned a great deal and he looked somewhat washed out. 'Den' remained a friend of Christian's, as did his brother, Gyles. Sometimes he joined Christian and Major Clough on a walk in the Home Park, a privilege extended to Military Knights when the Queen is not in residence at Windsor Castle.

Having contacted numerous people and pursued a great many lines of inquiry without success, I advertised for Denys Graves in the personal column of the *Daily Telegraph*. The advertisement drew no response. However, a conversation with Dawn Wood, daughter of Mr and Mrs Charles Keeler, directed me to Stratford, and with the help of a friend of his there, I was able to piece together his career.

Denys Graves was born in Essex in 1927 and was brought up with his mother and elder brother Gyles in Winkfield Road, Windsor. He loved his mother deeply. Once when playing tennis with a young friend, he saw his mother returning home in the car. He asked the friend whether she thought his mother beautiful and was most put out at the lack of enthusiastic response. She thought Denys 'rather precious'. Another childhood friend recalled, 'Denys was what would now be called *gay* . . .'

While his brother Gyles made a success of his life and married twice, Denys remained unmarried. He was a midshipman in the Royal Navy, then worked in the turnery department of Harrods between 1955 and 1957, selling broom handles and brushes. At another time he worked in a men's outfitters in Oxford. He claimed to be related both to the poet Robert Graves and the actor Peter (Lord) Graves. This has not been proven, but the former is not impossible.

In later life he worked in the theatre book store at the Royal Shakespeare Theatre, Stratford-upon-Avon. His colleague there, Irene Clark, remembered him as 'a cultured, artistic man' who knew his plays and loved the opera. He often sat and watched the productions and was a good critic. Mrs Clark recalled a portrait of Denys's mother, confirming her beauty. The rumour at Stratford was that Mrs Graves had tea regularly with the Queen.

Denys was considered 'a cut above the rest . . . a real character', largely happy, though given to moods. He took an annual holiday in the Canary Islands, staying in an hotel, which had to provide him with a south-facing room and balcony.

It would seem likely that Christian was a little in love with this man of matinée idol looks. Unfortunately Denys Graves is dead, otherwise he would have had much to say about the events that follow.

23

Years of Obsession

1960

Joan's friendship with Dick began gradually and gently, as these things often do. In June she wrote to congratulate him on a border he had designed. On her birthday in July she went to London to the theatre with him and Francie Kavanagh. Then Dick retreated to Ireland for a fortnight in August.

In September Joan began her correspondence with Dick in earnest, a long and prolonged series of outpourings that received few replies over the years. On 14 September, she invited him to 'give us the pleasure of your company for lunch and tea, or tea and supper'. A few days later she wrote again:

Dick dear,

Will you please wear the enclosed gloves when you are digging your 'gardens'? as I have stitched some oiled lint inside, greatly hoping it will help your bad finger, and do so hope you will not be offended at my sending them.

It was lovely seeing you on Sunday and shall look forward to that happiness again soon

With love & 'God' bless

from Joan

Dick's reply from The Links was kind but hardly encouraging:

Dear Joan,

Thank you very much for the gloves. It was most kind of

you, but I really feel you should not do this kind of thing, as I know these gloves cost a lot, & none of us are too well off these days.

And I really feel worried that you should have spent this money on me.

I hope you are well
    Yours sincerely
       Dick

Joan was not deterred:

Thank you very much for your letter this morn, which I loved getting, and knowing you were pleased with the gloves, but please don't be worried about my sending them, as it gave me so much happiness to do so, and I greatly hope that they will help your poor bad finger when gardening . . .

Blank days followed until 6 November, when Dick came to lunch: 'Darling Dick stayed for tea – and I felt very happy – Bless him.' On 17 December Joan wrote to ask him, 'Please may I see you *before* Christmas? Will leave it to you, to arrange the day . . .' Dick came round on 22 December, and a fateful day it proved to be. As we have seen, Joan recorded it in her diary:

Thank God – my darling Dick came this morn and brought his Christmas gifts, bless him. Heavenly seeing him. He is so *adorable* – and gave me the most wonderful kiss I have ever had in my life – blessed darling.

Dick did not appear on Christmas Day, though Major Clough was a guest at lunch at the house and Chris went back to Windsor Castle with him for tea. Joan wrote to thank Dick for 'that *lovely* box of chocs you brought us, it is such a *pretty* one, and so daintily tied up, bless you, and I love my little Rose Pin Box, which is adorning my dressing-table!'.

Before the end of that year there were two more encounters. There was a turkey dinner at Dargai, presided over by the now ancient Mrs Kappey, at which the guests were Dick, Francie and Billy Clough. The following night there was a party at The Links: 'My darling Dick was there, looking marvellous, as usual, bless him,' Joan recorded.

We can follow the story meeting by meeting until 1962, and through the letters a great deal further than that. Obviously the early years were the most significant, and of these 1961 was the most gruelling year for all concerned.

1961

In the New Year Joan's letters to Dick began to get more wayward and romantic. Dick received a poem on a slightly religious theme, sent on 2 January: 'Sigh not and say that no one cares . . . – I just had to send this to you Dick – as it's how you make me feel . . .'

Mrs Kappey was ninety on 18 January 1961, though Joan seemed more preoccupied with a visit to the pantomime with Dick two days later. In arranging this she told him: 'I am terribly sorry I forgot to thank you for coming on 22nd – but you must forgive me – as it was just because my Heart was so full of joy and Happiness at seeing you – I could hardly speak – cannot quite explain what I mean – but am sure you know . . .'

After the pantomime at the Theatre Royal, Joan recorded in her diary:

Simply Heavenly – my adored Dick came to the Pantomime

with me – and came here to dinner first, precious darling –
looking wonderful as always – and was *so sweet*, bless him. He
took me and brought me back in Little Minny Minor together, which was marvellous. The Happiest Evening.

That very night she wrote to him too: 'You looked super,
Dick . . . P.S. Please try not to smoke more than you can
help, Dick, because of your cough . . .'

According to the calendar that she marked each day, Joan
saw Dick only thirteen times in 1961. The dates in this calendar were marked with a circle. This was not for lack of
invitations from Joan to Dick, suggesting that he come over
for lunch, tea or supper. These were mingled with injunctions that he stay indoors and keep warm and avoid risking
'flu by being out in the damp garden. In February Joan
invited him to come one Saturday or the Sunday following.
Dick made his polite excuses: Maurice O'Connor had died,
there was his funeral, then he was planting shrubs at Bices-
ter, and so on.

Joan replied: 'It was lovely to see your handwriting, but
needless to say, am *very* disappointed you are unable to
manage either Sat. or Sunday – however, shall look forward to
the happiness of seeing you as *soon* as you can manage it. Will
you let me know any weekday for supper, or the first Sat. or
Sunday, you are free for lunch and tea, as that would be
lovely . . .'

Joan continued to invite Dick and he continued to fend off
the invitations. She besought him to spend Easter with her,
but his mother was coming over: 'She has so many friends
and relations, her visit will be very hectic.' Joan was philo-
sophical: 'I shall at least have your handwriting with me at
Easter.'

In February 1961 Joan put Dick's name on the Prayer

Circle through the Seekers Trust. Simultaneously she asked that the name of her former friend, Jimmy Hill, be removed. Based in Kent, the Seekers Trust described themselves as 'the Guild of Prayer and Spiritual Healing'. They held 130 circles of prayer each week, each lasting for half an hour. In the 1960s some 9,000 people were 'linked' by saying the same prayers at the same time wherever they were. Joan's link time was 10 p.m. on Sunday evenings, so at that time, faithfully, she went to her room and prayed in silence for Dick. For this service, she sent the occasional postal order for half-a-crown.

More than that, the admirable secretary of the Seekers Trust wrote encouraging letters, urging Joan to be positive, commiserating over dry rot and assuring her that 'our prayers will protect your dear Mr Bonham'. She pointed out that of the 6,000 servicemen 'linked' in the last war, only two had been killed. Joan remained a loyal supporter of the Seekers Trust for many years and drew sustenance from the association.

Joan was inclined to telephone Dick, though she became a bit nervous if other residents of The Links answered the telephone. She felt she was more sure to reach him by letter and relied on his good manners to reply. Socks were sent to Dick for Easter and he thanked Joan for these: 'I am wearing them at the moment & they should last for a very long time.' This reply, wrote Joan, 'meant more to me than the Queen's Crown Jewels would have! Was delighted to know you were pleased with your socks and were wearing them when you wrote, bless you.'

In April Joan invited Dick to the ballet in London on the day after his birthday: 'Could we go there and back in Little Minny Minor, please Dick? and I thought perhaps get a "snack" in London before the Ballet, which starts at 7.30 – as you must have something after a day's work. It will be Heavenly if you can come.' Joan told Dick that she had not mentioned her little plan to either her mother or Chris. But no, Dick wrote that he was 'booked up'. Joan was sad 'beyond words':

> I did *so long* to. Anyway, can I book you for next year, darling? It's so difficult having to carry on as usual, when one is feeling sad, Dick – am afraid I have been living in a dream – all today with *you*. I so often do, because it helps me – till I see you again . . .

Joan began to buy vitamins for Dick and for herself and a feature of their friendship from now on was her regular sending of these to him wherever he was from wherever she was. Then there followed a St Christopher to look after him in his many travels by car. By June Dick was flagging and failed to refuse Joan's latest invitation. Joan's next letter was a mixture of rebuke and pain:

> Dick darling
>
> I have felt sad – beyond words, all day, that you did not let me know, whether you could come to lunch today, or *next* Sunday – it was so unlike *you* – I thought you would ring me this morning, and waited till 11 o'c. before ringing you, in case you were having a rest on Sunday, but *alas*, when I did so, Giles [Howard] said you had just gone out and would not be back till late this evening – and I had got you a very special lunch too –
>
> Dick – I hope with all my heart – you were not cross with me, for asking if you would like me to ask you to Geoffrey's & June's [Bourne-May] little party too, were you? Anyway I humbly ask your forgiveness – for whatever it is, as I would not lose your friendship – for the World. You must know that

– Dick – Greatly hoping that you will give us the pleasure of your company next Sunday – My love . . .

This was normal behaviour for an obsessed person. First she played on his guilt. But, unwilling to face the cold truth, she gave him the benefit of the doubt. Then she looked to the future.

Ascot Week loomed and Joan went over to The Links to help park cars with the group. She was happy. She saw Dick twice. And then there was Miss Kavanagh's party to thank the helpers and she saw him again. But the holiday season threatened and Dick was due to fly to Ireland. Joan was determined that he would come and see her before he went, as 'there is something I *must* tell you – before you go'. She insisted that he had promised to come.

On 6 July there was a new development. Joan had dreamt up a new name for him: 'Dick – "My Knight in Shining Armour" – I have christened you this – as it is what you *are* to me & so appropriate for you . . .' Joan invited him over, of course, and told her mother about it: 'I told Mother I had asked you – Dick, and she says she will be very pleased to see you.'

But Mrs Kappey did not see Dick. She died on Sunday 16 July, an event that is not recorded in Joan's little calendar – somewhat unusually, given the family's respect for death and its various anniversaries. Joan's absorption with Dick seemed to smother the significance of her mother's death. It is possible that both Joan and Christian felt the need to latch onto other landmarks of hope, Dick and Major Clough, as their mother's life ebbed away. At any rate that is what happened.

Joan wrote to Dick at The Links, giving him the sad news, and he rang to offer his sympathy. Even at this traumatic time, she did not relent:

Joan and Christian at a London wedding

Aunt Clare marrying Gus Hughes-Hughes at the
Brompton Oratory, London, 1933

Neville De Rinzey – a
boyfriend who disappointed

Mrs Kappey aged ninety, in the garden at Dargai

Christian at Dargai – Joan reflected

Major Billy Clough at work in the garden at Dargai

The man with matinée idol looks – Denys Graves

Dick Bonham – up against the garden wall

More Kappey guests up against the wall.
(*Above left*) Lady Dorothy Palmer in old age, (*above right*) the author
in his youth, (*below left*) Christian with Denys Graves,
(*below right*) Lieut.-Colonel Reggie Kappey

Joan with Smokey Velvet in the garden at Dargai

Dick darling –

Thank you – for your sweet sympathy – it was dear of you – to ring me at once, when you got my letter, but just like you – and it is beyond me to tell you – Dick – just how much it meant to me – to hear your precious voice. It gave me help and courage I *most* needed, as I longed with all my heart – for *you* to be with me – and that was the next best thing.

It has been an awful shock and strain for us both – as you can imagine and I fear will be, till after Friday – but all our friends have been kindness beyond words – and we are so thankful Dick – that poor darling Mother's passing over was *so* beautifully peaceful . . .

Two days after the death, on 18 July, Mrs Coad, the next-door neighbour, was looking out of her window in the way that neighbours do, and observed a tall fair gentleman call at the house, emerging from a cream van. Joan was out when Dick called and very distressed to hear that she had missed him. She rang The Links in an urgent panic and Francie told her that Dick was out. She suggested that Joan come over there for lunch on her birthday (20 July), but Joan was deter-mined to have Dick to herself. He did not fail her. He appeared on 19 July at the house.

Joan wrote in her diary: 'Thank God – my darling Dick came & spent the morning with me, bless him – was adorable, & I took 2 photos of him.' It was fascinating to discover that it was on this occasion that Joan took the two snaps that were soon converted into the two lasting major icons at Dargai, reprinted and repainted, adorning every wall and corner, multiplied all over the house in their dozens. As we shall see, the snaps were converted into portrait photographs, hand-coloured to her specific instructions, some copies achieving a better quality than others.

Joan took the visit as huge encouragement, thanked God for it, and wrote to Dick:

> I have *never* in my life – felt as I do and you *must* believe this – I simply love and *adore* you – and always will as long as I live, Dick – but I am some years older than you . . .

Dick then crossed to Ireland for his annual visit to Woodville, his aunts' dilapidated house, for the Dublin Horse Show, a number of dances, and to help with the large house-party that the Hamilton sisters were entertaining in true Irish style. Daily letters from Joan greeted him in the hall when he came down for breakfast, not to mention his supply of vitamins. Joan also sent him copies of his photographs and gave her opinion of them:

> The one in the garden is *lovely*, Thank God – and is being such a comfort to me Dick – as I've had it enlarged, and it is life-like, on my dressing-table – *unfortunately*, the one in the drawing room is a bad light – one side of your face – it *is* a pity, as I always love to see you sitting in that chair – and it's so good otherwise, but please darling, will you let me try again, when you get back from Ireland?

Joan started to doodle at home, writing 'Dick and Joan', and later their names and his address, endlessly on bits of paper and generally incorporating his name with hers.

August was a tricky month for Joan as she could not contact Dick and was anxious to do so before she and Christian went to Scotland for a recuperative break with old Mrs Alexa Bourne-May and then a visit to one of the aunts in Glasgow. She hoped he would be home before they left. Finally she rang The Links, where Louis Murphy told her that Dick was still away. The two sisters then entrained for Scotland and after a difficult journey found themselves housed in unaccustomed splendour at Barwinnock, Kirkcudbright.* Joan had something positive to relate for once:

> On arrival here I got quite a shock! as it's an absolute *Palace* of a house in about 30 acres of gorgeous woodland etc. My bedroom is enormous with a huge four poster bed in which I feel completely lost!! There is the most *lovely* view from my windows across woodland & fields to distant mountains purple with heather.

Joan enjoyed her break and rather dreaded the return to the house in Windsor. Soon after her return in September Dick lunched at the house and was presented with a tie and some socks. But Francie was there too, and so Joan could not tell Dick the many things in her heart. However, she continued to telephone The Links, sometimes several times a day, and to write her letters. Eventually Francie rebuked her and tried to make her see reason. On 25 September Joan poured out her heart to Dick:

> My very dearest Dick,
>
> I am feeling desperately heartbroken and unhappy – you will know why – To *me* you will *always* be my 'Knight in Shining Armour' – as a wonderful dream of Happiness – I prayed with all my heart – would come true – as I just adore you and to *me* – it will always remain sacred – but as *your* Happiness is my greatest wish – this is to humbly ask for your forgiveness, if I have been worrying you – with too affectionate letters – according to Frances – and for *devoted friendship always* Dick – as you simply *cannot* go out of my life – I must be able to see you often *please*, as great Pals – and do

---

* Christian was much taken with Mrs Bourne-May's beautiful cream-coloured Jaguar. She asked if she could drive it and she promptly crashed it, causing a certain amount of damage.

things for you sometimes – and I very earnestly ask your *help* – in this remaining happiness Dick. Please forgive my writing this letter. I just had to – and thank you – darling, for the greatest happiness in my life – for a short while – I shall never forget 22nd Dec. as long as I live Dick.

My devoted love – and God – and my St Christopher – always keep you safe for me

Yours ever

Joan xx

To this letter Dick sent a reasoned reply:

My dear Joan

Thank you for your letter. It is sad to think that I have been the cause of making you happy & unhappy & that you should have built up quite such a picture around me.

I hope that in future, we may remain as ordinary friends, which will mean that I shall be able to go & see you both, in the way that I always used to, when I first came to live here & that I shall not have to make a point of being away, when you come to visit The Links, & it grieves me to have to 'be away' to any of my friends.

Pray to God & let him lead you his way, & I know you will find peace. I never pray for anything direct that I think I would like or I feel I should have in order to make me happy.

Pray around it, pray about it, & let him do the rest.

Yours

Dick

By return Joan thanked Dick for writing: 'I'm so thankful you wrote yourself Dick – and will endeavour very hard – to fulfil what *you* wish – as my great longing is to grow like *you* – as I think you have the most lovely forgiving nature – and you have brought me nearer to God than I have ever been Dick . . .'

Any hopes that the correspondence would cease or the pressure diminish were short-lived. Joan was chastened for a time, but when she renewed her campaign, her first approach was an expression of despair:

> I feel there is nothing to live for now – as you know, *you* mean more to me than anyone in the World – and always will. Please pray for me – I feel so utterly heart broken – and help me by giving me the happiness of seeing you *soon* – in devoted friendship as I shall understand. It's frightful having to carry on feeling as I am . . .

Joan took comfort in visits to All Souls Church, Langham Place, the church of the BBC, which she knew to be a favourite haunt of Dick's. She could not resist sending him a postcard of it. This was the first of several solitary visits she made there.

About a month after she was warned off worrying Dick, Joan was allowed to help him discuss new shrubs and rose trees and work with him in her garden: '. . . and then I helped my precious Dick with our Border – just *Heavenly* – a wonderful dream come true – Through the love of Jesus – then we had tea – and he stayed till about 7 p.m. bless him'. Any hopes that this might calm her down were in vain. It merely rekindled her hope, 'and made me want to live'. She longed to help him again.

A sudden visit to the house from Denys Graves, the man with the matinée idol looks, was another excuse to make contact with Dick. Perhaps she hoped to make Dick jealous. Yet Denys did not like Dick and, at about this time, he made some unpleasant remarks about him. I do not know what these were, but they need not have been particularly hostile to arouse Joan's anger. He might have described Dick as a confirmed bachelor or told Joan that she was pursuing a lost cause. He might have implied that Dick was rather hopeless.

Thereafter Denys was *persona non grata* with Joan. With angry biro marks Joan obliterated Denys's name from a diary note about his tea-party with her mother in March 1960. Again with what appears to be some anger, Joan scratched out a reference to Denys in one of the last letters that her mother wrote to her.

Dick did not respond to Joan's mention of Denys. Instead Joan paid another visit to All Souls Church. Then she heard that Dick had been ill and she could not let that pass. She resumed sending the vitamins, at the same time asking him, 'When can we finish the border, Dick?' Shyly she concluded, 'I hope Frances will not be too cross with me – for writing – but I know *you* will understand I had to – and forgive me Dick and I am sure she will too.'

The next two encounters took place at The Links at the behest of the understanding Miss Kavanagh. Francie invited Joan to tea to meet Dick's aunt, May Hamilton, and Dick himself arrived 'late for tea and looking as marvellous as ever, bless him, and was a darling'. Joan was delighted to meet his aunt: 'I thought she was so sweet & so clever to paint those pictures so well', but she went too far as usual: 'I couldn't quite believe it was really *you* – when you walked into the drawing-room, bless you, but I knew God would bring you. It all seemed like a lovely dream – which alas ended far too soon . . .' Ten days later, Joan was again at The Links. Francie asked her to stay on and Dick returned from his day out in Oxford while she was still there:

Thank God – once more – for another lovely Happiness – of spending the evening with my adored Dick, at dear Francie's. It was a truly Heavenly surprise as he arrived in time for dinner, and we were together all the time till 10.30 when he, blessed darling, and Francie brought me back – alas – and my dream of happiness was over – till next I am with him – He looked wonderful and was adorable – and God in His Love grant I shall be with him again *very soon*. It was marvellous – how He brought him to me and *will* do again – *soon*.

Joan cooled down a little, but then became haunted by the fear that she might have upset Dick by turning down his offer of coffee – the excuse for another letter. Presently she sent him a tin of chocolate biscuits and mints for the car, lest he should feel peckish while working through the lunch-hour, and some blackcurrant pastilles in case his cough troubled him. On 27 November she wrote:

Have I been rather selfish in writing to you too often? If so, I humbly ask your *forgiveness*, and understanding, Dick – because adoring *you* as I do – I long to write every day – and know how you are – as you are *always* in my thoughts and prayers – and each day seems like weeks to me . . .

Jealousy was never far away either. Patrick O'Grady introduced Dick to Mr and Mrs Charles Keeler* at Sefton Lodge, Winkfield Road, and Dick tended their borders. Mrs Keeler sent Dick a book on ornamental trees and shrubs. When Joan heard of this, she sent him a different copy and urged him to use hers instead.

Christmas was harder for Dick to escape, and the invitations to share the day with Joan began to arrive early in December. Joan hoped he would come to lunch – 'Am afraid we shall be quiet, Dick – being the first one without Mother.'

---

* It was Mr Keeler who had rescued Joan from Holloway Sanatorium in 1955.

Meanwhile Christian was making better progress with her friendship. Major Clough was expecting her for tea and evensong at St George's Chapel. Joan sent Dick a silver heart and cross and Dick was routed from his lair, briefly, a few days before the holiday. He went to Clarence Road with his gift in the afternoon, catching Joan employed in cleaning the windows. They had coffee together and she presented him with a jersey, tie and handkerchief. Dick stayed a mere half-hour and then sped on his way to St Albans. Joan had wanted to declare her love for him but had been restrained by a warning from Miss Kavanagh at lunch that day, 'which hurt me *terribly* – though I shall *never* believe it was wished by *you* to be said', she informed Dick later.

In the end the Christmas season proved a good time for Joan, from the point of view of sightings of Dick. These were becoming scarcer and she was having to savour what she could. Francie Kavanagh and Louis Murphy came over with Dick to dinner but left early, while Dick stayed gallantly on till 11.15. On 30 December Francie arranged a pantomime treat for sixteen people: 'I sat by my dearest Dick – who looked & was adorable, bless him. We had coffee together at half time – and then we all went to the Chinese Restaurant for dinner after – thank God – I sat near Dick – precious darling.'

On 2 January 1962, Dick again dined at Dargai, on a freezing cold night, and drank Joan's Ovaltine before he left at 11.08.

1962

The year 1962 saw the pattern established by which Joan and Dick were by and large kept apart. The mastermind behind this endeavour was Miss Kavanagh, gently but loyally supported by the inmates of The Links. Nothing they did was done with spite. On the contrary, what they sought was a *modus vivendi* that kept everyone as happy as possible under the unusual and trying circumstances. Therefore Joan was allowed to visit The Links on certain defined occasions. By 1970, when I knew a bit about the story of Dick and Joan, it seemed to me that Ascot Week and the Christmas season were such times and that on these occasions Dick resigned himself to his fate. Otherwise he could be relatively confident that Joan would not be invited and thus The Links was his home and his haven.

The telephone was a problem, but Dick rarely answered it and the others covered for him if Joan was on the line, as of course she very often was. As for the letters that rained down daily on the front-door mat, they certainly served as a constant reminder that she was never far away.

Joan's 1962 calendar again records some thirteen circled dates, times when she saw Dick. The rest were struck out sadly, one after another.

It would be pointless to quote at length from the 1962 letters, which continued in the same tone as those of 1961, becoming more desperate as Dick remained silent. But there were several alarming extensions to the obsession during this year. First, Joan became anxious that her letters were not getting to Dick, so she took to registering them at what must have been mounting expense even in those days.

Joan was aware that she was being a nuisance and frequently asked forgiveness and described herself as being naughty in writing. By this time Dick was not bothering to read the letters much, so he ignored the various invitations that showered on him. Joan duly telephoned, hoping that there had merely been a delay in the post. When Miss Kavanagh answered the phone, Joan was thoroughly ticked off. She explained to Dick:

I tried to ring this morning but Frances answered and said you were out – and sounded rather cross Dick – because she said I had been writing too often to you again. Perhaps I have – for which I am *truly* sorry Dick – and earnestly ask your *forgiveness* and understanding, once more as you have been so *perfectly* sweet in helping me – but as I said once before the days just seem like years – in between my seeing you . . .

Then came the terrifying message she always relayed to him and which proved to be true:

Dick – you can *never* go out of my life.

The anniversary of the evening at the pantomime was on 20 January, and Joan invited Dick to dine. A new ruse of hers was to say that she would expect him unless he told her he could not come. He did neither:

I have just been in a dream with *you* – all the evening, and waited and waited, and prayed so hard – that you *would* arrive in 'Little Minny Minor' – as you never let me know you could not come, and I said in my letter, will expect you, unless I hear to the contrary – I had a lovely fire, and supper ready for you – which was not cleared away until 10.30 uneaten.

Far from rebuking him she then threw herself once more on his mercy, introducing a new theme – that she did not mind how 'badly off' he was.

In February she decided to take a positive step to ameliorate Dick's finances, writing a private letter to her bank manager:

Dear Sir,

Will you please transfer £200 from my account to Captain Richard Charles Bonham's credit account – as R. Section, which is his branch, tell me you can do this for me, without my writing a cheque – as I wish it to be *strictly anonymous* will you please make *sure* of this and get it done as *soon* as possible, letting me know when completed – thanking you –

Yours faithfully

Joan Kappey

The bank manager from a smart branch of the well-known bank where they both held their funds duly replied:

Madam,

We thank you for your letter of 23rd February, and as requested have transferred the sum of £200 from your account No. [. . .] to the account of Captain Richard C. Bonham with our R. Section. This transfer has been made anonymously as you request.

The worst of this was that Joan's account was now left with only £155. 13s. 1*d*, so she could not afford this generosity. Somehow the transfer went undetected for three whole years.

The letters continued and Joan's took on a more desperate tone as Dick failed to respond to invitations and appeared not to be at The Links when she rang up. Joan even tried the line that Mrs Keeler was feeling let down because he had not put her rose trees in 'but as you did not let her know, she has got someone else to put them in.* What a pity, darling, as you told me you were going to do them. She said she wd. still like you to get some lupins for her border Dick . . .'

Joan saw Dick following a three-month gap at the end of March. The occasion was a Grand National party at The Links, after which Dick drove her home and stayed at Dargai for an hour. Joan was thrilled and there was a letter to 'Sir

* Patrick O'Grady stepped in to plant the roses.

Richard', her 'precious Knight in Armour' from 'the Lady Joan'. More letters ensued and the telephone calls resumed. Joan's next meeting with Dick occurred because the precautions taken at The Links went wrong. Joan was there on 27 April and naturally hoped to see Dick.

Dick had gone to London by train, they told her, but then he walked into the room. It was an agonizing situation. She had to go in to dinner, leaving him in the chair in the drawing-room. But his birthday came round again, an excuse to send him a gift. Dick replied:

My dear Joan,

Thank you very much for the pullover, but you really must not send me any more presents.

If you do, I really will have to return them – & would do so whoever they were from. Surely you can understand this – & how difficult it makes things for me.

Hoping you are both getting on well with the house.

Yours very sincerely
Dick

Joan would not be deterred, though: 'My heart leapt for joy when I saw your precious handwriting – which I have longed to do for *so* long – but Dick darling – I *implore* you not to say I mustn't make you any more presents . . .' – all of which was followed by much more of the same.

The annual ceremony of the Order of the Garter was to take place in June and Major Clough offered Joan tickets. She invited Dick: 'I shall *not* go unless you come too, I simply *couldn't* face it . . .' Dick would have liked to watch the procession, but not on those terms.

In June Francie invited the sisters over and Joan informed Dick: 'Just to tell you, we are unexpectedly lunching with Frances tomorrow, and please God, and you – I shall have the happiness of *you* being there. Am afraid deep down, that is why I am coming Dick, though of course it will be nice to see dear Francie also . . .' She was lucky that time: 'a Heavenly day with my adored Dick. We were so wonderfully *Happy* together, and He was so *adorable*, bless Him', though another resident described as 'that wretched L.M.' (possibly Lady Mant) 'planted herself' beside them. Joan wrote: 'The only thing I shall *never* forgive myself for is that I did not *kiss* your darling little curls on the side of your *precious* head and open my heart to you as *you knew* I was *longing* to Dick. Why did *you* say I shouldn't?' As a result of this, Francie took the stern measure of informing Joan that her help would not be required parking cars during the Royal Meeting at Ascot.

In July, Joan turned her attention to the two photographs she had taken of Dick a year before, just after her mother's death. She sent both of them away to be converted into colour portraits, with highly specific instructions about the colouring. The garden photograph, her favourite, was to be coloured as follows: the eyes blue, the hair light golden brown, the complexion light suntan, the shirt white, the tie light maroon, and the coat light fawn background with bluey-green and brown check. Dick's trousers were to be dark grey and his shoes brown suede. His buttonhole was a deep red rose. The flowers in the garden were blue larkspurs with red roses and green foliage.

The indoor picture was submitted to the same process, the colouring of the chair cover described to the minutest detail.

In August Dick retreated to Ireland and Joan became worried when Miss Kavanagh came round to see Chris and told Joan that Dick was not sure if he would be returning to The Links. A predictable panic ensued. Ominously, Joan wrote to Dick that she had been busily doing up her side of the house in preparation for his arrival to live there.

On 25 August she did something far worse. She altered her will in such a way that if she died, her sister Christian would find herself part-owner of Dargai with Dick owning the other share. She also severed a joint tenancy agreement she held on Dargai with Chris 'so that I am able to dispose of my share, as I wish, or be able to sell at any time'.*

Had Dick been an unkind man, he could then have forced Christian to sell her share and take half the proceeds of the house for himself. Joan wanted to leave him her diamond and gold star brooch and her five-stone ruby and diamond gold ring, her holding of £500 Defence Bonds and her share of the furniture and furnishings of the house. Mercifully she did not die while this will was extant.

In September she contemplated the first of several trips to Ireland, making inquiries about staying in the Lucan Spa Hotel, not far from Woodville. She did not go, and was greatly relieved when in due course she 'gazed at' Dick's 'darling face' once more.

In December, after a frustrating autumn of silence and few meetings, Joan was able to confront Dick and declare herself to his face. She was satisfied with the reaction that he said he was 'not cross' and her campaign sailed forth into the new year.

1963

Dick was in Ireland with his mother for New Year, and Joan eschewed the festivities at The Links, unable to face them in his absence. It was an exceptionally cold winter, and England

---

* In a letter to her lawyer, dated 11 August 1962, Joan reduced a bequest of £300 to Christian to £100.

lay encased in a mantle of snow well into the spring. Neverthe-less, the pantomime at the Theatre Royal was performed as usual.

Why do the victims of obsessions behave inconsistently? Dick had more than made his point and was ignoring the various letters, invitations and injunctions that bombarded him. Yet somehow the victim can rarely let go completely. Unpleasant as it is to be bombarded with daily calls and let-ters, it has a compelling side. Nothing is more worrying than when an obsessed person falls silent. At least Joan did not torture Dick in that way.

In all the circumstances it is surprising to find Dick writing from Woodville in Ireland, responding positively to Joan's in-vitation to the Windsor pantomime:

> This brings my best wishes for 1963 – Thank you very much for your kind invitation to the Pantomime on Jan. 18th – I shall be delighted to go to it – & I hear it is very good this year. I am trying to get back to England, but we are com-pletely snowed under at the moment, but I have booked a flight for Monday 6.30 p.m. I hope the planes will be flying by then. Have had a v. busy time – Dick.

Why did he do it? Did his mother say he should go? Was it *such* a wonderful production of *Cinderella*? On 14 January Joan wrote to Dick's mother, whom she had met but once, sending her one of her prized photographs – a 'snap I took of your darling Dick in our garden'. She addressed the letter 'Dear Dick's Mother' and added, 'It was so nice speaking to you when I phoned, but needless to say I felt *very* sad that Dick was out. With love, may I? as somehow I feel I know you . . .'

Dick caught his flight and returned safely from Ireland. Joan interpreted this as more than a good sign: 'You spoke volumes by coming all that way back to *me* from Ireland, blessed darling Dick – on 18th in that frightful cold weather – to have tea in "our room" and dinner together – and then the pantomime all so *truly* happy.' Joan chose to believe that Dick had fought through the snow and blizzards to reach her as a pledge of his love for her and that now all would be well. Seeing him on the doorstep made her both happy and afraid. From now on surely all would be well. Alas, not.

During these years Joan and Christian lived at Dargai together. In the absence of the dominating presence of their mother, it might be thought that the two sisters could have relaxed into a happy and mutually supportive friendship. Sometimes this was the case, but not always. There were tensions in the house, brought on by the breakdown of the family, the continual worries about paying bills, Christian's realization that her sister had embarked on a self-destructive mission and her own somewhat unconventional devotion to Major Clough.

Because not all the Kappey papers survive and in particular most of Christian's papers had been thrown away in Joan's lifetime, it is not possible to trace Christian's every move as I would have wished. Likewise I cannot monitor exactly what she thought of Joan's quest at this point in the story, although I am able to do so later on.

Christian had begun to nurse Major Clough during a winter illness, from which he recovered well enough for a visit to the pantomime with her. Christian was not yet living in Major Clough's house, though she spent much of her time there. At Dargai, the two sisters repaired their old home as best they could, eliminating dry rot, and they then divided their territory. Joan took possession of the sitting-room at the front, Chris the room behind. Joan was on the first floor, Chris up at the top of the house. When they were on good terms, the arrangement worked well.

Chris's old Major was still marching into St George's Chapel gallantly and gamely in his Military Knight's uniform. He managed to do so until late 1967, and only after that did Christian's nursing of him become more intensive. In time she moved in with him, caring for him constantly as we have seen. There is something noble about the way she coped with her old boy, and the way he responded. It cannot have made Joan's plight any easier.

In March Joan pursued Dick to the Orangery in Holland Park in London, where she knew he was working. She came from Windsor in pouring rain in quest of him and walked through the gardens, searching everywhere. Finally she spied his much beloved shabby form, digging away. He was working for his friend, Jim Russell. Naturally she ran to greet him, thanking God for the discovery.

A drama in the summer revolved around Major Clough's Garter party. Their brother Reggie and his second wife, Eileen, were over from South Africa and Joan tried to book Dick's company well in advance. She had a particular reason to be worried:

> Dick – for God's sake – help *me* by coming on June 17th. I do implore this – as I now hear Major Clough has invited that wretched fellow Denys Graves to his party, & Chris will be bringing him back here – which means I shall be compelled to admit him to 'our room', a thing I haven't done for nearly a year now, as I am afraid I *detest* him Dick. He has said some horrid things about you. Quite frankly I never want to see him again! . . .

Joan was true to her word. She never forgave Denys Graves and would not even speak to his brother on the telephone.

Denys had denigrated Dick. There could be no greater crime.

Joan refused to go to the Garter ceremony because Major Clough did not invite Dick. She was furious. She retreated into dreaming about him: 'you were by *my side* and *my arm* through *your* lovely strong one'. In her panic she expressed herself with bitterness: 'Do you know it is *six months* since *you* last *blessed* the threshold, & *my* heart with *joy* Dick.' But Dick did not stand by her side. Joan complained:

> My adored Dick,
>
> I trusted *you* with all my heart to come and be *with me* this evening in *reality* darling. I felt certain you *would* Dick. I *implore* your forgiveness wherever I have failed you . . .
>
> Unfortunately I *had* to tolerate that Graves fellow in 'our room' with the others but I *never* spoke to him, & came up to my room as soon as our cousins left about 9.30 . . .

The invitations and rejections went on and on. If anything, the letters and calls got worse. It was like a Hitchcock thriller – the pressure on, then the pressure off, then on again. Joan saw Dick on her sixty-second birthday on 20 July and she put her arm through his in the garden at The Links. A tie was sent to him, and a chain to wear round his neck always – symbolic she said, of love, but he must have thought of it more as symbolic of manacles that bound him. Dick then went to Ireland, and when he was home again, Miss Kavanagh announced that he was out. Joan was in despair. She wrote to The Links and sent an identical letter to Woodville. So where was Dick?

Mairi O'Grady, Patrick's widow, was able to solve this mystery for me:

> When Dick disappeared, he was, by then, a great friend and godfather to our youngest son, Roderick, who was born in

1960. He came to hide – i.e. park his caravan at our cottage in Thorpe, near Egham. In the end we had to kindly ask him to leave as it all began to look very scruffy . . . Poor old Dick felt the cold, of course, so he usually returned to The Links in the winter.

Nine months without sight of Dick meant that 1963 was rather a gloomy year for Joan, and almost another month passed before 15 November, when, after trying all afternoon, she accidentally reached Dick on the telephone. Thereafter she rang often but Dick was either 'out' or 'away'. He must have lived in a kind of hell, unable to answer the telephone in person, hiding behind the other inmates of The Links, and fending off the barrage of unwanted gifts. Undeterred and yet unsure of his movements, Joan made a Christmas pudding and ordered a turkey. Hopes were dashed when a letter from Francie announced that he was off to Ireland for the Christmas holidays. Still she persisted, sending him a card with a robin on it: 'I have the dearest little robin *just* like this one, that comes to me every day & I have called him Dick!' In his absence – a single sighting that year – Joan again boycotted the party at The Links. 'I simply couldn't face it without *you* being there – I know I should break down . . .' But she was given 'new life' when she reached him on the telephone on New Year's Eve.

1964

The 1964 calendar tells a yet sadder story. The occasional days that are ringed indicate days on which Joan heard Dick's voice. It may be that she did not see him at all that year. Joan sent Dick a sheepskin coat (with his initials in it) and began the year by buying tickets for the pantomime on 22 January. She urged him to wear the new coat on that special occasion. A few days before the proposed date she rang his mother's home at Woodville. Lily Bonham told her that Dick was not there and nor was she certain whether he was still in Ireland.

On the day of 22 January Joan took the Christmas turkey out of cold storage and that evening she cooked it for him. She also cooked the Christmas pudding and brought out a delicious cake. She lit the fire in her room at the front and she waited. Dick's picture was all round the room, the portrait of Aunt Clare presided haughtily above the sofa, and Harry Jacob and his mother were in their silver frame. But Joan felt solitary. Dick did not come and the tickets were unused. They still exist and were kept with the letters, the tear-off section intact. Joan confessed she was '*dreadfully sad*'. Then she did manage to talk to Dick and was distressed to hear that the sheepskin coat had been detained at the Customs on its way to Ireland and, worse still, that Dick did not feel he should accept it anyway. She implored him to find it in his heart to accept and wear the coat. In February Dick sent the coat back. Joan felt 'utterly crushed'. Nevertheless she sent him a gift that was in the coat's pocket and continued to hope that he would change his mind about it. Eventually Dick relented and accepted the coat, which he wore till the end.*

By March, it was a year since she had set eyes on her beloved idol. At last, in April, she could bear it no longer and went round to The Links and waited for him outside. After two hours he came out – 'our Angels of love *brought you* out in the end'. Courteous as ever, Dick gave her a lift home in 'Little Minny Minor', but this marked a sinister development. A few

* Mairi O'Grady recalled, 'We ended up with the coat and it fell to bits on my student sons.'

days later, on his birthday, Joan tried it again, rising at 6 a.m. and making her way to Ascot in dawn's cold light. In her hands she bore her presents. She waited outside the gate, like a hopeless waif in a Dickens novel, until suddenly his car swept out and bore him away.

According to Joan, he never saw her. Of course he saw her. When he was safely gone, Miss Kavanagh emerged from the house. At first she was angry, but she soon pitied the cold little person and invited her in for a cup of coffee and showed her round the garden. Joan left her birthday gifts at the house for him. This time Joan also wrote to Miss Kavanagh:

> I feel I must just write & thank you again so *very* much for being so sweet and kind to me on Friday when I was feeling so *truly sad* – at not seeing my darling Dick on his birthday. I *longed* to ask you if I might stay till he got back but as you did not think it would be until late evening, I did not like to impose upon your kindness dear, though I was *desperately longing* to . . .

But Joan had gone too far this time, and Miss Kavanagh once again told her that she did not require her help in parking cars at The Links for Ascot that June. On 16 July Joan's obsession found yet another outlet. She placed a memorial notice in the *Daily Telegraph*, under the name of KAPPEY. It read: 'July 16 1916 and 1961. Mother and Harry. Till we meet again – Reggie, Chris, Joan and Dick.' Dick would have been surprised to have been included in this touching tribute.

Joan's next worry came when Dick went to Northampton to work there for three weeks. Nor did she succeed in obtaining his address. Her despair was now so great that she resorted to sending him packets of cigarettes, while begging him not to smoke too much. When a postal strike occurred, Joan delivered her letter by hand, leaving it on the chest in the front hall of The Links.

Dick was either at Woodville or in Northampton, Joan did not know for sure, but when she reached Lily Bonham on the telephone she heard that his Aunt May, the artist, had died suddenly. May was painting right up to the end: 'What a grand way to go,' wrote Joan in sympathy to both of them, recalling her one meeting with the aunt at The Links.

A new idea preoccupied Joan. She wanted to know exactly when Dick was born. She duly wrote to the Registrar General at the Customs House, Dublin, 'as I am *very* anxious to *know* for *private* reasons'. A postal order for 8/6*d* was sent and in time she was rewarded with a copy of Dick's birth certificate. This proved he was born in 1916. Now she owned a bit more of him.

On 21 September, Joan transferred £20 into Dick's bank account, anonymously. By October he appeared to have disappeared completely. He was not at The Links, nor was he at Woodville. He might have been in Northampton. Joan wrote to him via his bank: 'Oh Dicky – for God's sake let me know how and where you are.'

There was never a sign of Dick. Joan went to the wedding of her cousin Virginia, the daughter of Audrey Long (who, with her brother Geoffrey East, occasionally helped Joan and Chris financially).* This was a rare excursion for Joan – 'I made a terrific effort to go':

> Virginia had a very lovely wedding. Needless to say – *you* were *by my side*, every minute of the time *my Dicky* – with my arm through *your lovely strong one* – which I certainly needed

* Virginia Long married Captain Michael Arnison-Newgass, 3rd Green Jackets, The Rifle Brigade, at St Michael's, Chester Square, on 5 December 1964. The reception was held at Claridge's.

darling – as there were over 200 guests I believe. The flowers in the Church were *beautiful* Dick – & I longed for *you* to see them too – all white lilies & chrysanthemums arranged in the shape of a Christmas tree – & as Virginia & Michael knelt at God's Altar – it was *you & me, my adored Dick* in my heart & soul & my first & last toast – was to *you & me, my wonderful Dick*. There wasn't a soul in the room, who could hold a candle to you *darling Dicky*. I kept my piece of wedding cake for *you*, which I enclose . . .

Near Christmas, Dick returned to Ireland where his mother needed him to support her following the death of his last aunt, Connie. Joan wrote to sympathize with her: 'My darling Dicky's Mother, I hope you will not mind me addressing you thus – but "Mrs Bonham" sounds so stiff!! when I adore Dicky . . .'

Her frustrating quest for Dick continued. This time she telephoned and his brother left her on the end of the line while he set off to find Dick. Time passed. Eventually she hung up and rang again but received the engaged signal. The telephone was off the hook.

1965

It may be that Joan's resolve in keeping copies of her letters began to flag, or maybe there were some bundles that got lost. From now on, fewer survive, but the story can still be told. The New Year began with Joan alone in her room at Dargai knitting a jersey for Dick. Just before midnight she went out into the garden and stood 'under God's star-lit Heaven', her arm linked in fantasy with his. Dick's silence was prolonged and was not interrupted by the festive season.

Sadly her obsession had led her to send out Christmas cards signed by 'Dick and Joan'. Their friend Geoffrey Bourne-May was taken in by this, writing back:

> We imagine that something splendid must have happened at Dargai since last hearing from you & Christian – & does this mean, in the old-fashioned way of saying it, that you & Dick have 'an arrangement'? We all felt awfully silly, as we had no idea until your kind cards & calendar arrived, so you must think it dreadful of us never having written before this. My Mamma wanted to write to you straight away as soon as she got your card, but then thought she should wait in case you had something in the papers . . . It all sounds *too* thrilling.

When news of what Joan had been doing began to circulate, Dick's mother wrote to Chris complaining that she had coupled her name with Dick's. Chris was embarrassed and concerned. Joan admitted she had 'got carried away by the heavenly thought of our *really being married*, darling'. She apologized.

I wondered what Mrs Bonham thought about it all. It would appear that she did not worry unduly since she did not consider Joan a particular threat to Dick. Joan would never marry Dick, though there were other candidates that Mrs Bonham might have been more concerned about. Even so, Mrs Bonham probably did not know a fraction of what was going on. Joan's papers contained endless meandering scrawls: 'Dick and Joan Bonham in our little home together & at Ballintaggart, Colbinstown, Co. Kildare.'

From Joan to Dick went an endless stream of hand-knitted jerseys (both high-necked and sleeveless) and socks, bottles of rose-hip syrup, and Vitapointe hair cream. She dispatched liniment lest he cut himself shaving, St Christopher medallions, peppermint creams and Bemax, and even evil cigar-

ettes, besides the habitual letters, backed up with telephone
calls. So many of the letters were the same, word for word and
line for line, and only occasionally did the world's news merit
a mention: 'Sad to think poor old Sir Winston has passed on –
what a great man he was.'

It is the occupational hazard of those with limited resources
that from time to time they receive a letter from the bank
manager courteously pointing out a shortfall in funds and
asking the client to declare his intentions as to when he will
speedily rectify the unfortunate situation. In the 1960s such
letters were even sent out when the amount overdrawn was
less than ten pounds. Dick must have received many such a
letter, but for a while his bank had been enjoyably quiet. At
this time, though, Dick was in touch with his bank and he
made the disagreeable discovery that certain sums of money
had been transferred into his account. He was very upset.

It will be recalled that Joan had transferred some money as
long ago as February 1962. On 17 February 1965 Joan transferred a further £20, again instructing the bank manager: 'I
wish it to be *strictly anonymous* please.' The manager did this,
acknowledging, 'We have noted whilst transferring this money,
for it to be strictly anonymous.' But on 16 March, the manager
wrote again, informing Joan that they had been 'asked by Mr
Bonham to refund this amount to the donor'. He added: 'We
would mention that this sum was passed anonymously to Mr
Bonham.' Joan replied:

> I write to say I was *most distressed* & amazed to hear about the
> transfer of the £20 to Captain R.C. Bonham's account. If it
> was done *strictly anonymously* as I *requested* – *how* in the *world* did
> he discover it? It is most mystifying . . .

The bank reassured Joan that 'Captain Bonham queried
the credit and when told it came from an anonymous source

he asks that it be returned'. Joan then asked the bank manager for other ways that she could credit money to him without his detecting it: 'How very tiresome of him to query the credit of it!!' The manager took the kind of step for which bank managers in today's computerized age of business have scant time:

> The point you raise is rather a difficult one to deal with by correspondence, and I am wondering if it would be possible for you, next time you are in Town, to call and see me so that we could discuss it and I could give you the benefit of my advice. I hope this will be possible.

But Joan then heard from Dick and thus replied:

> Actually there is no point in my coming up to town, now, to discuss the matter I asked your advice over, as Capt. Bonham has told me *himself*, that you *informed him* on the *telephone*, as to *who* the *donor was*, which I was *very amazed* and distressed to hear about as you had *assured me*, you would keep it *strictly anonymous*, & on *no account disclose it* – as *I know he would never permit it*, if he knew – & I quite thought you would adhere to *my wishes*.

Meanwhile Dick had gone to the Hebrides to assist Jim Russell in laying out Lord Granville's garden at Callernish House, on the island of North Uist.* From there he wrote to Joan on 5 April:

Dear Joan,
    I had reason to check up on my Bank a/c for Income Tax assessments, & I have discovered, that you have been transferring money from your account to mine.

* The Granvilles remember Jim Russell, but not Dick.

I have written to the Bank & told them, that they are never to accept money from you, to be lodged in my account.

I know that you considered this to have been a kindness from you to me.

But I can truly say that it was a very foolish act – owing to the fact that your income is not a large one – & money which you possess is provided to run your house, & to keep you & Christian, in as much comfort as possible.

I have arranged with the Bank, to transfer £50 back into your a/c & today I have asked them to transfer another £20.

I hope to pay off the £200 before very long & so to give you back the £240 which I owe you.

I do implore you to give up sending these presents – & to get on with your life – separate from me.

You have so many friends – it is a pity you don't reach out to them & forget this silly infatuation for me.

You have built up a very false image of perfection around me. Few of us are perfect, & I fall short of it all, by a long way.

I do ask you, *not* to send any more presents.

Many of your friends have very rightly told you of the line to take.

Do follow their advice & mine. This has all been a very great worry – to me – & to your friends.

So again I implore you to give up this pointless venture.

Yours

Dick

Joan's response was the same as usual; a telegram sent to Lord Granville's address: 'DICK THANK GOD YOU HAVE ARRIVED SAFELY – MY LOVE JOAN (THANKS LETTER, WRITING)'. But the letter she then wrote does not survive.

Joan's next project was one she had nurtured since 1962, and possibly longer. She would go to Ireland in the summer and see Dick on his home ground. Then all would be well.

Joan's plans did not run smoothly. As early as May the Powers Royal Hotel in Kildare Street was fully booked for the mid-June/July season. Had she been able to go there, the cost of a taxi from Dun Laoghaire would be approximately 14s., they said. Then Joan wrote to Dublin's famous Shelbourne Hotel to reserve a room. They were again very busy but informed her that to reach Colbinstown, Co. Kildare, there was a bus that left the city each evening at 5.30 and she could be there by 7.35. The Shelbourne proved to be full during the crucial time.

Joan kept in touch with the Powers Royal Hotel and in July she settled on a single room with private bathroom and breakfast from 5 to 15 October. She sent a deposit of £3 and asked them: 'Please order some nice fine weather! as it's the first time I've been to Ireland'. The manager wrote back: 'We shall have pleasure in ordering some fine weather for your first visit to Ireland! Hoping that you may enjoy your stay with us . . .'

In September Joan booked her passage on the ferry. She would travel 2nd class on the train from Euston and 1st class on the boat (a single-berth cabin with toilet). Meticulously she marked down the various times and costs.

But on 30 September Joan lost her nerve and cancelled her plans. The Powers Royal returned her deposit of £3: 'We are sorry to learn that you are ill and have to postpone your first visit to Ireland.' She sent £1 back as compensation for the loss of the room. Then she undid all her other plans. She never went to Ireland.

On 27 November Joan sent Dick an Irish pound by registered post. He returned it with a sharp note on the envelope: 'I have *told* you not to send these presents.'

1966–1969: The Elusive Pimpernel

The next few years followed in the same vein as the previous ones, Dick keeping his distance. At one point, when Dick yet again failed to answer, she wrote: 'I think I shall have to christen him: The Elusive Pimpernel.' On 20 December 1966, Joan wrote the letter quoted at the beginning of this book:

My adored Dick

Exactly six years ago, *this Thursday* Dec. 22nd – *your dear lips met mine* – in that *blessed & wonderful kiss* ever there and sacred – for it awoke *my very soul Dick* – and made *you mine* and *me yours* in *my heart*, as long as I live, whatever happens. No one has kissed them since – or ever will *Dicky* – as long as I remain conscious. I told you this once before and I repeat it – and mean every *word* I say Dick. *Please* believe this – in the sight of God – As ever at Christmas, & as the New Year dawns – and every day of the years to come, my Heart will be *with you, close to yours* my Beloved Dick, as I love & *trust* you till you make it real . . .

By the time the story reached 1967, I found that the lives of the Kappey sisters were about to be interwoven with my own, though it would be another two years until we met. Joan recorded a visit to the Windsor Horse Show in May 1967, and reading the letter I recalled vividly that I had been there myself. It was the occasion of Prince Andrew's first solo royal engagement:

I *longed beyond words* for *you* to be *really with me Dicky* – as it was such a gorgeous floodlit evening session with the Mounted Bands of the Life Guards & Blues, & the Musical Ride by the R.H.A. with the gun carriages was too glorious for words! with the Castle floodlit in the background. The Queen arrived in the ring & in the afternoon little *Prince Andrew* presented the cups & rosettes to the Services Teams with great confidence! & he looked so sweet! . . .

In June 1967 Lily Bonham lunched at Dargai for the first time, brought there by Miss Kavanagh. Joan struck up something of a correspondence with her, informing her in October that her friend, Lady Dorothy Palmer, the deaf old lady I met at their house in 1969, had suffered 'quite a nervous breakdown, suddenly, poor dear, owing to financial worries and is in a most ungettable at hospital, just outside London, unless one has a car!'. Joan offered Mrs Bonham the hospitality of her home if The Links was ever full up and 'if it wouldn't be too humble for you!'.

In 1968 there were three meetings in total between Joan and Dick. In 1969 amongst the usual letters was a card bearing the Queen's portrait in the uniform of Colonel-in-Chief, Irish Guards: '*Dick.* Her Majesty *Commands* that *you* should *come* as *soon* as possible – as I must see *you* again soon. I told her how I *long* for that *Joy – My adored Dicky* – and she said she would send a *special Messenger*!! commanding that *you come* – I wonder if the Royal Warrant has reached you yet?!!'

Even a mock summons from the Queen failed to bring Dick to heel.

24

Reggie's Rebukes

I never met the brother, Reggie. He had rather dropped out of the story after his divorce from Dolly. He remarried some time after the war to a lady called Eileen, who had grown-up children and in due course grandchildren. They lived in Kenya. Thus he played little or no part in the lives of the Kappeys. He was never a particularly sensitive fellow, nor a man of more than a few words.

Reggie had retired from the Army as a Lieutenant-Colonel, and was now serving as supervisor of the Nairobi Forces Club. Kenya passed through the difficult Mau-Mau period while he was out there. He was never quite sure when he might have to bail out. He dreaded having to return to England; he had enjoyed warm climates for so long. He kept busy, was grateful for good health, but bemoaned relative impecuniousness. 'What wouldn't I give for a bit more of the necessary, as we have to count every penny?' was one of his refrains.*

The death of his first wife in 1969 was something he took in his stride, and he was similarly abrupt when he nearly lost his second wife: 'Eileen got a go of cardiac asthma the night after she arrived here [Pietermaritzburg] & had to be carted off to

---

* In December 1966, Reggie sent Joan £1 for Christmas, declaring, 'It's all I can afford this year.'

hospital at 3 a.m. I thought she was going to die as she couldn't get her breath . . .'

None of Reggie's letters to Christian survive, but from his letters to Joan, he sounds as though he was more naturally in sympathy with her than with Chris. He worried that the two sisters did not get on well together. He hated hearing hints of the tensions that occasionally arose between them. Most of all he worried about Joan's introspection and her obsession with Dick. In March 1964 he wrote to Joan summing up their situation, as was his way, in terms both simple and matter-of-fact: 'Chris seems to be going places & I wish you would too, but anyway my dear that is your affair. If you are happy that is all that counts & we both hope that things will come right one day, who knows.'

Reggie was not alone on the African continent. His mother had a number of younger sisters and his aunt Marjorie was out there at that time. But they fell out, each describing the other as wholly impossible, and as Reggie said, 'She is the most impossible person & was d—d rude to us which finished my friendship as far as I'm concerned & when I have finished with someone it's final.'

In 1966 Reggie and Eileen moved from Kenya to South Africa, probably to avoid the difficult political situation. From his new home at Gordon's Bay, he remained the adjudicator between the two sisters. At this time Chris was living in Major Clough's house, so Joan was alone at Dargai:

[Chris] says you have been marvellous to her & it did me good to hear it as I hated to see you bad friends. I hope you learn to keep each other, without any malice as it would be a blessing to me as basically you are two grand women.

I only wish you were all in all to each other as this is a grim world today.

However I'm sure it will all pan out right providing you both are sensible.

Reggie did not care much for Major Clough, then an ailing 93-year-old: 'I have my own opinion about Billy as you know.* Still it takes all sorts to make a world.'

A month later Reggie mused on the problems of Joan's role while Chris nursed her old Major: 'I must say I think you are d—d good the way you look after things alone at Dargai. Chris does appreciate it I know but it doesn't alter the fact that it all falls on your shoulders.' A little later he added: 'Billy is a b—dy marvel & thanks to Chris hanging on to life. I hope she doesn't take it too badly when he goes. I have told her several times to brace herself for the inevitable. I only hope she will when the time comes.'

In January 1970 Reggie remembered Lady Dorothy Palmer and contemplated the role of Dick in Joan's life:

Am glad you see a lot of Dorothy. She is a darling & you seem to see quite a lot of Dick. Wish that could come to something. Who knows? Can't his mother influence him a bit? Anyway I pray for you in that respect as I feel you deserve it.

Yes Billy is a marvel & I only hope Chris doesn't work herself into the grave as I don't think he will reward her for all her love & attention. We will see.

In 1970 Reggie suffered a stroke, from which he made a good recovery. Able to wield a pen once more, he reassessed the plight of his sisters once more that June:

Am glad you had a session with Dick as I know the pleasure

---

* 'He's an old so & so as you know' . . . 'Chris is an idiot over Billy, but what can you do?', etc.

you get from it & after all that is the main thing in life to get a bit of happiness where you can. It's a shame it doesn't develop beyond that stage as when you get older it's the real companionship in daily life that one really wants apart from the security side, & neither you nor Chris have really had that. Such a pity. Billy is a d—d marvel, but I'm afraid when he goes Chris is going to feel the draught & I only hope she doesn't have a complete breakdown. But as I have told you there is always a bed for either of you here as long as we're alive . . .

Neither of the sisters ever made the journey to South Africa, however. In February 1971 Reggie underwent a serious stomach operation, which he survived. He became very thin, with a failing appetite and a scar nearly nine inches long. He lost thirty pounds. On 9 March he wrote, 'Don't worry as beyond having ½ my stomach removed they say I'll be fine in time. God bless & best love, Reg.'

Reggie died peacefully at Doon, Gordon's Bay, exactly a year later. The two sisters united to add some words to Reggie's memory on their mother's grave in Windsor Cemetery.

25

A New Decade

Joan must have wondered how her obsession with Dick would end, while Dick must have hoped that with the passing of the years the pressure would diminish. That turned out to be partly true, but neither of them can have guessed that it would end the way it did.

I witnessed the ending myself as I saw a great deal of them both during the lifetime of old Major Clough and in the months after his death. There were long gaps, of course, while I travelled and while for the academic year of 1970/1971 I attended Strasbourg University. But once you were a friend of the two sisters you were a friend for life. We always exchanged Christmas presents and they wrote me long letters while I was away. In those days I was a better correspondent than I am now, and I wrote back often myself. Rereading these letters, it is impossible not to be warmed by the kindness they showed to a youngster who appeared in their lives. I am haunted by the feeling that I was not as good a friend in return, though there is no hint that they ever thought that.

One letter from Joan has taken on greater significance since I began to write this book. In the summer of 1970 I was 'depressed' in the way teenagers often are in those difficult years when their futures are unresolved. I believe I spent a great deal of time being 'depressed' in those years, worrying about love and life and what to do. I wrote to Joan and mentioned my plight somewhat repetitively:

> I wrote to Christian recently to say that I'm off to Cornwall with friends today and it will be a real tonic. Poor me has been feeling very depressed this week. Without doubt it has been the worst week for a long time. Never mind, Cornwall will be an excellent tonic! I expect we all have these weeks from time to time . . .

Joan wrote back:

> Dear Hugo,
>
> Thank you *so* much for your nice letter, which I was *so* pleased to get with news of you – and how sweet of you to write, just as you were off to stay with friends in Cornwall. I was so *very* sorry Hugo dear, to hear you had been feeling depressed, and quite *meant* to have sent you a line sooner, to say, I do so hope you are feeling heaps better dear, but it's awful the way the days go by, & I never seem to do half I want to! There is so much to cope with in the house & garden! without any help, so please take the will for the deed! Yes, indeed, I think we all get depressed at times. I know I do! and then I say to myself 'Thank God – for your many blessings, and the love and kindness of dear friends and relations' and I feel better . . .

These words say much more to me than they did at the time, knowing, as I do with hindsight, what Joan was enduring. I understand her and I marvel somewhat at the contrast between the clear and thoughtful way she offered comfort to me and her earlier somewhat desperate and despairing communications with Dick.

Shortly after Major Clough's death in September 1970, Christian returned to Dargai after an absence of two years.

Joan had struggled on by herself while Chris had been away nursing. A letter from Joan to a friend bears the familiar disapproving ring of her mother: 'It has literally been "non stop" for me what with the garden and the housework to cope with single handed for 2 years . . .'

During the early 1970s the flow of letters and cards to Dick did not abate. And there were still calendars throughout the early 1970s with dates ringed with hearts to denote sightings and meetings. In 1973 the markings in one such calendar were inscribed: 'Thank God, my beloved Dick' – month after month. Joan always waxed lyrical about any encounters with Dick or visits to The Links.

Joan still communicated with Dick in the same romantic tone: 'As the New Year dawns *Dick*, my *Heart* will be *close* to *yours* – and my arm through *your* lovely strong one.'

Coincidences have played many parts in this story. The first meeting that I ever had with Dick at the home of Mrs Sadleir was an extraordinary one. Thereafter there were many more, some at The Links, but most at Dargai, lunching with the Kappeys. (In June 1974 Dick was at lunch and talked a lot about his family. Joan wrote to me afterwards: 'I fear we did not have much chance to hear about *yourself* . . . owing to Dick's "House of Hamilton"!!', but she must have been pleased at the ease of chatter at her table, and that he was there.)

At about this time, I had an unexpected sighting of Dick in London. In those days I lived in Egerton Terrace, just off the Brompton Road, and was returning there with some friends lateish on a Saturday evening. Dick's 'camper' was parked next to a pub called 'The Bunch of Grapes' on the corner of Yeoman's Row. He was by the door and I recognized him at once. He recognized me too, I am sure. He looked different from the other times and I felt I had caught an uncomfortable glimpse of another aspect of his life. We did not speak, nor did we ever refer to it. Maybe he had just paused to pick up a packet of cigarettes?

This story must not be about my friendship with the Kappeys or indeed Dick, but a few things are worth recording. Looking through my old diaries, I can determine exactly when I saw them and sometimes more than that. I went often to Dargai for Sunday lunches or teas. I invariably called in on Christmas Eve on my way to the Carol Service at St George's Chapel, sometimes delivering a brace of pheasants donated by my father. But as time went on, I confess I went less often.

There were reasons for this. First, my life became busier, and after 1975 when I became involved in the research of my first biography,* I went most weekends to Northampton. Then I remember one Sunday lunch at Dargai in December 1973, which was so cold that I could see my breath at the table. I came away shivering, frozen virtually to the bone, and had to go to bed at home for several hours to warm up. Selfishly I resolved thereafter to visit in the summer rather than the winter, but then of course there tended to be more tempting invitations elsewhere in the summer.

There was another problem that arose as the 1970s progressed, which made visits to Dargai something of a strain. Joan became more difficult. She had always been rather jealous of Chris, and it was sad to find the two sisters bickering even when guests were there. Chris was really my friend, but Joan would become annoyed if one went into Chris's sitting-room rather than hers.

Laughter and joyful chatter had been a feature of a visit to Dargai in the past. Game resilience against adversity had

---

* *Gladys, Duchess of Marlborough* (Weidenfeld & Nicolson, 1979).

sustained the two sisters as they surmounted the problems of living in a large, unmanageable house without the income to support it. It was depressing that as they aged they became bitter towards one another, though never to their friends. I found it an uncomfortable situation. So I went there less often.

26

The Plight of Lady Dorothy Palmer

It is hard to think that there were yet others who were in a worse plight than the Kappey sisters themselves. One such was Lady Dorothy Palmer, the deaf old lady I met on my first visit to Dargai.

The Kappeys loved to entertain and did so whenever their limited funds permitted. Essentially their lives were dull, but from time to time there was a visit to the Windsor Horse Show or The Links. But their inherent goodness meant that much of their energies were taken up in the care of such sad old folk who needed their help.

Some of the characters dropped out of their lives by death – Dick's mother, for example, died in November 1971, aged eighty-seven. But Lady Dorothy Palmer continued to go to lunch every Sunday from Barn Cottage in Oakley Green.

There is no doubt that this was the highlight of Lady Dorothy's week, but it cannot have been rewarding for the Kappeys. As Joan described it in 1970 to Lady Dorothy's brother, Lord Cecil Douglas: 'Darling Dorothy comes here for the day most Sundays as I hate to think of her alone so much, especially being so deaf. She seems pretty well on the whole . . .'

I met Lord Cecil at lunch at least twice at Dargai. He had been one of the few family mourners at the funeral of his uncle, Lord Alfred Douglas. I liked him and was in awe of the things he knew and the way he cast off fascinating information about Mrs Dudley Ward and other figures who were part of history to me and yet an everyday part of his world. He was easy to talk to.

He came to lunch out of duty as the Kappeys were so kind to his sister. Sometimes he took them out to lunch. He would collect Lady Dorothy on these occasions, but there seemed to be little conversation between them. His wife seldom accompanied him and I never met her, though it appears she directed matters from afar in a number of very long telephone calls. He was, in conclusion, a social man, a member of White's club, and he led a very different life from his sister. I may be unnecessarily harsh, but I think less of that pair now, reassessing the position from the occasional letters and postcards they sent to the Kappeys. In this I am not alone, since during Lady Dorothy's old age, one of her neighbours offended them by saying they did not do enough for the sad old lady.

In September 1973 Lady Dorothy suffered a bad fall and spent three weeks in Windsor Hospital. The Kappeys visited her without fail every day. Thereafter she was put into St Mark's Hospital in Maidenhead. 'We are most distressed about it,' wrote Christian. Lady Dorothy was able to come over for Christmas and partook of some of the pheasants I had brought. In June 1974 Joan reported that Lord and Lady Cecil Douglas had brought her over for tea: 'I got an awful *shock* when I saw her. She looked so *ill*.'

Lady Cecil Douglas was forever at pains to communicate how much she and her husband were doing for Dorothy. In one Christmas card she noted that they would be with Dorothy 'some part of Xmas Day', adding, however, that Lady Dorothy was expected to lunch with the patients in hospital. There followed some gush about Joan and Christian being 'wonderful true friends', as indeed they were.

As long before this as 1968, Lady Cecil Douglas had defended her position regarding Dorothy's finances. On heavily embossed writing paper she explained to a concerned neighbour in Oakley Green that Dorothy had £287 in the bank and £20 in her bag. Evidently this was considered ample for her needs as she had some income from shares, occasional handouts from the family and 'a good meal from m-on-w [meals on wheels] every day except Sunday & except for the cat there is little to buy'. Lady Cecil went on to point out that the family were doing enough and were not 'by any means well off'. Lord Cecil gave his sister £4 a month. However, she did mention that a property company might pay out a large dividend the following year, in which case they would do something more.

Meanwhile postcards were sent by the Douglases from Switzerland, Padua and elsewhere. These holidays and their home in Green Street and later Chesham Street must have been expensive to maintain. It is lucky that Joan and Christian were on hand to help poor Lady Dorothy.

Lady Dorothy returned home to her cottage in December 1974 and was cared for there, with occasional visits to hospitals when her helpers needed time off. Christian still went regularly to fetch her in her little car and take her home again after lunch, an expedition that became increasingly tiring as they all got older. Sometimes Christian bathed her and put her to bed. Christian summed up her attitude to Dorothy in a letter to me: 'O, dear, what a tragedy old age is and what a "comedown" to the Marquess of Queensberry's daughter.'

Eventually, Lady Dorothy was transferred to the Ascot Nursing Home, next door to The Links, where she died on 12 March 1980, aged eighty-five.

Old age took its toll on the Douglases. Lord Cecil spent his last days driving up to a nursing-home in Hampstead to visit his wife, who had become a patient there. Finally, on 26 February 1981, he killed himself, fearing, erroneously, that he was dying of cancer. His wife followed him to the grave in the same year on 9 May.

I have looked up their wills. While Lady Dorothy left a mere £14,617, Lord Cecil left considerably more – £119,035, and his widow £73,246. In conclusion, the Kappey sisters were Lady Dorothy's best friends.

27

Christian's Tale

> She spent hours writing nonsense to Dick
> – *Christian's diary, 28 August 1973*

Of all the documents that I have, the one that gives the clearest impression of life in the Kappey household at around this time is Christian's day-to-day diary for 1973, the only one of its kind to survive.

The fact that I was now a small part of the Kappey world and they of mine means that there is considerable mutual ground. I find that I too was a character in this diary, just as Joan and Christian frequently figured in mine. A particular example was especially interesting to me for what it revealed so many years later.

I discovered that both Christian and I had recorded an outing in our respective diaries. In a little five-year diary that I used to keep, I noted on 13 February 1973:

> Down to Windsor for lunch with Joan & Christian. Then to Ascot to see Chris's paintings & met Mr Lonsdale Bryans. Tea at The Links.

My diary also reveals that this was an oasis of time away from another problem that was concerning me enormously at the time, but that problem I did not share with Christian. Interestingly, on the same day, she wrote:

Hugo coming to lunch, & to see the picture exhibition. He came & was so sweet. I ran him over & introduced him to Jim who was very intrigued with him. Took Hugo back for T. Francie playing bridge. I left soon after 8.45.

But the ever cheerful Chris was likewise worried about other things, of which I knew nothing at the time. Her diary continued:

J. in awful mood, keeping the Tierneys' cat. O God, I think she is not at all well, am worried to death . . .

So we were both distracted, but neither showed it on the day.

In this one diary written by Christian, much of it records letters received, excursions here and there and problems over money, overdrafts, and pensions. The Links played a greater part in Christian's life than I had realized. She visited the inmates several times a week. Equally the care taken of Lady Dorothy Palmer was of prime importance, and she too, I note, was taken over to The Links from time to time.

During 1973, there were several dramas which upset the daily routine at Dargai. There was growing tension between Chris and Joan, one problem being Joan's habit of imprisoning stray cats and making them her own. Evidently Joan shut Mrs Tierney's cat in the front room and had to be prevailed upon quite fiercely to give it back again. But the next day Joan had imprisoned it again, a situation which ended with the cat becoming part of the Kappey household.

On 17 January Christian noted: 'Joan went shopping – has started writing reams to Dick again.' Rows followed, ending with Joan telling Christian to get out of her room. The reason for this became clear a few days later when Joan accused Christian of 'trying to run Dick'. Christian commented, 'She is getting highly hysterical over nothing.' Yet the hysteria continued, as did the rows. By 22 February the jealousy over Dick and the drama over the cat led Christian to comment: '. . . hope she isn't going to have another break'.

There was also jealousy from Joan's cat, Smokey Velvet, who resented the arrival of the new cat and thus came to call on Chris until Joan discovered his disloyalty and shut him up too. Chris's diary is full of friendly visits to her from Smokey. On 21 March Chris was writing, 'J. in a *devilish* mood & sprayed the place with her stinking poison', and yet worse a few days later: 'unprincipled bitch, Joan, is buying whisky & having it every night'.

Chris was aware that Joan was jealous of her, and this was confirmed years later by Betty Worthington. Chris made friends easily, was popular and had a giving nature. She was prettier too, with blue eyes and a pale complexion. She had the same benign look as the Queen Mother, and never an unkind or suspicious thought in her head. Yet when it came to her sister, she was worried and judgmental. Once in her diary she went further than usual and attempted to block out the words. These I deciphered: 'It is very shocking to think J. is taking to drink at £4 a bottle. She wants her bottom smacked.'

Towards the end of April, Christian began to worry about Joan's expenditure of electricity as she sat up late into the night, knitting Dick an unwanted birthday jersey. The relative calm of Dargai was at length shattered on Tuesday, 15 May:

Did the shopping, got cats food – had devil of a row with J. about drinking. She bashed me in the face, so I gave her one back. Luckily I was able to escape to Francie, the garden looking really beautiful. O dear, how sad life is. Wish darling little mother was here or my darling Billy. Perhaps we will make it up. I hope so . . .

A week later I dined at Dargai with Louis Murphy and Francie as the other guests, Christian noting, '*horrid* joint, but everyone seemed to enjoy themselves'. Little did I know what had been going on a few days earlier. This evening was sandwiched between further horrors, Joan upping the intake of whisky, Christian warning her about how their brother Reggie had been a victim of drink, and Joan becoming increasingly irritable. In October Christian wrote that her mother had appeared to her in a vision, calling out, ' "Stop Joan." Please God she has the sense.'

Despair, leavened only by her natural optimism in life, kept Christian vital and active. She was worried to death about her sister, now dubbed 'the dragon', and often prayed for the strength to go on. At this time Sir Edmund Hakewill Smith prevailed on her to return Billy Clough's Military Knight cloak. Both sisters subsisted by selling little objects here and there. Occasionally one of their many aged Mills aunts or uncles left them the odd £100. Expeditions kept Chris going; she enjoyed the kindness of a tight-knit circle of close friends.

On 1 July 1973, Gyles Graves, brother of Denys, the man Joan so disliked, rang up, but unfortunately Joan answered the phone. Gyles was no more popular with Joan than Denys. She told Chris she was 'wanted on the phone by a man', and then listened in, behaving, as Chris put it, 'like a ruddy lunatic, in fact a really wicked woman'. Gyles, somewhat more successful in life than Den, told Chris that he had remarried, was leaving Chelsea and going in for antiques in Dorking.*

* Gyles Graves eventually moved to Walberton, near Arundel in West Sussex, where he died on 18 February 1990. Meanwhile Denys got as near to the stage as was ever likely by working in the theatre book store at Stratford. He was still there in the mid 1980s. He retired to Cheltenham, where he died of a heart attack on 29 May 1988.

It would be pleasing to note a change as the year went on, but sadly the situation deteriorated. By November Christian was writing of Joan: 'The dirty little beast is still drinking whisky, & I *pray God* she realizes what she is doing & give her strength like Reggie, who was wonderful . . .' Chris became nervous of even being in the same house as Joan.

The year ended equally badly. Chris saw Dick at The Links after Christmas 1973 and noted: 'Poor Dick looks *very* much on edge. Hope he isn't going to have a breakdown again.' Thus 1973 drew to a sorry close.

During these years the only way this situation altered was by gradual deterioration. Money was scarce, the house decayed and so did the health of the two sisters. There were quite a number of falls, and other minor domestic accidents.

Eventually something happens that changes everything and that was to happen in November 1976. Little did the Kappeys know it as they sat down to a lunch for sixteen at The Links on Christmas Day 1975, but time was running out.

28

Knight's Move

There was much sadness in store for the Kappeys in the latter months of 1976. First, Louis Murphy died peacefully on 16 June, following a heart attack, at Ascot's Heatherwood Hospital, poignantly on a day when the inmates were parking cars for Royal Ascot. The inmates guessed correctly that he was eighty-five. He proved to have a nest egg of over £23,000, which he left in trust for Francie. Worse news reached me in a letter from Christian in November:

> Did you see the death of our most darling friend, Francie Kavanagh? It was in *The Times*. It was a most *tragic* end to her wonderful life. She was found dead, on the floor of her bedroom – on the 11th of this month. We shall miss her more than words can tell. For so many years we have been a part of 'The Links' – and had so much happiness & fun. We cannot bear to think 'The Links' will be empty next year.

Joan added to this: 'Wasn't it too *sad* about poor darling Francie Kavanagh, & dear Louis Murphy? We miss them *so* much. There is such a blank.' And Dick Bonham, to whom I wrote a line of sympathy, filled in the gaps:

> Francie's death came as a great shock to us all. She had been playing bridge the afternoon before she died & also been watching the television with us till 11 p.m. The following

morning she didn't appear at breakfast at 9 a.m. & at 9.10 Mrs Knight who was 'helping out' went into her room & found her lying on the floor. She called for me & I felt her pulse but got no beat. She had dressed & made her bed, so she must have died instantly between 9 & 9.10 a.m.

A wonderful way for her to go – But we do miss her dreadfully, & the Links will be closing down on Dec. 19th when Andrew Kavanagh [her cousin] collects the furniture which is going to Borris, their old home in Ireland. I have been here for 22 years & Francie has been my greatest friend & adviser all those years. A horrid feeling having to start a completely new life.

Chris & Joan have been over quite often. They are not looking at all well. Joan has got cat mania & now has 9 cats & I think all their money goes on feeding cats & not themselves . . .

. . . I hope we will meet again before long . . .

Francie Kavanagh left £47,443, and in her will she bequeathed £1,000 to Dick 'in memory of all the help he has given me over the years'.

All the inmates of The Links headed off to new destinations, some of them to nursing-homes, the plight of many sad old people with no one to care for them.

Lady Mant had died some years before. I had been intrigued by her unrelenting silence at table the day I lunched there in 1970, and also by her habit of walking alone each afternoon around the lanes near Ascot racecourse. I often asked Christian about her, but all she was able to tell me was that she had left The Links. While researching this book, I discovered that she had gone to White Lodge Nursing Home in Maidenhead, where she died in June 1973, just before her ninety-eighth birthday. She was relatively well off, leaving a number of diamonds and other jewels. A year before she died she cancelled her will and then revoked the cancellation with a new codicil, so clearly she was still able to take decisions. Her silence at the table was probably due to extreme deafness rather than caprice, a rather disappointing conclusion.

Of the other inmates that I knew, Jim Lonsdale Bryans shuffled off to Hellesdon Hospital, near Norwich. He became a victim of senile osteoporosis and senile dementia. He died in the hospital on 25 January 1981 aged eighty-seven, leaving so little that no one bothered to take out a grant of probate. Tod Body went to Ridgemead House, the nursing-home in Englefield Green, and died there in June 1985, aged ninety.

Dick was obliged to move out. First he went to The Red Lodge, Englefield Green, the home of his friends the O'Gradys. But he did not stay there for long, as Mairi O'Grady recalled:

> He was a lost soul. The Links was his life. He seemed to prefer to be on his own, muddling along in his own way. We never wanted his caravan parked in our garden, tucked away in a corner. Anyway it was winter-time and we didn't think he should live in a damp caravan. He was only really with us for about six months.

During this time occasional letters still arrived from Joan. Dick never spoke of the situation, but Mairi O'Grady was well aware of it. She recalled: 'He would get a few letters, I do seem to remember that. He'd give a rueful smile, and roll his eyes.'

This enforced change of circumstances was Dick's opportunity to make a move and escape from the long persecution he had endured. I wondered what he would do. Surely he would now distance himself from Joan and her letters –

possibly succeed in disappearing completely? Joan did not stray far from Dargai on account of her cats. She hardly went beyond the local shops. She would never find him. Besides, she was older and her determination had considerably diminished.

Would Dick return to Ireland, where he would be welcome amongst the huge network of his Bonham and Hamilton cousins? Would he perhaps follow Jim Russell to Yorkshire? Jim Russell was now busily and successfully engaged re-creating the gardens at Castle Howard. Or would he just travel about, taking pot luck where he could find it? There is always work for a gardener, and Dick was partly nomadic by nature.

On the other hand, his friends were largely in the Ascot area or settled nearby in Berkshire. Patrick and Mairi O'Grady were in Englefield Green, and even if he did not live there, he could always count on a square meal. He had other friends at Binfield, and his last official address was given as 'The Caravan', The Priory, Binfield, Berks. But did Dick really live there? Where was he most of the time?

The most fascinating part of the long drama between Joan and Dick is the way it ended. Nothing could have surprised me more than to discover that Dick had moved in with Joan and Christian. It was amazing. He who had spent a decade and a half avoiding Joan, refusing to answer the telephone, neither reading nor replying to her letters, became the mainstay of Dargai, 159 Clarence Road.

Why was Dick there? 'It was really because there was nowhere else to go,' recalled Mairi O'Grady. Dick finally succumbed to the relative comfort that Joan could offer him. He was welcome at Dargai. There was company of a sort, food and alcohol, and a modicum of heat.

Behind the large garden at the back of Dargai was yet more

land, derelict and neglected. There was a large garage, and both the derelict land and the garage could be reached by an unmade track that ran behind all the houses on the north side of Clarence Road. It was there that Dick encamped, parking his van on Kappey land. There, basically, the van remained.

Dick would come into the garden through the door in the castellated Victorian stables and enter Dargai via the kitchen. Whether or not he stayed in the house in mid-winter, I do not know, but he was a feature from then on.

I visited the Kappeys on Christmas Eve in 1977, not having seen them for over a year, and this is what I noted in my diary:

> Joan opened the door. I dreaded an over-affectionate embrace. She seized me and kissed me so hard it almost bruised me. Then she left me alone while she went about making tea. Dick Bonham appeared and later Christian too. I always think she's the best.
>
> Dick Bonham now lives in a caravan on the ground at the back. He says he feeds the Kappeys as best he can but really it is desperate the way they feed twelve cats but not themselves. He is always keen to talk and this time it was to be all about 'Bibs' Plymouth,* whom I've met. He said the Plymouths were rich, getting income from mines, docks and yards in Wales. Yet she was always a bit socialist. She could be very informal or extremely grand. She preferred the informality of St Fagan's† though. He waxed lyrical about her and wanted to see her again.
>
> Joan produced tea very late. I struggled to eat the requisite before pleading an excuse to run off to the chapel [St George's Chapel] . . .

* Irene, Countess of Plymouth (1902–89).
† St Fagan's Castle, the Plymouths' home near Cardiff.

A further diary recalls that I lunched with the Kappeys in January 1978, not long after this. By then I had observed how unkind Joan was to her sister: 'There are always undercurrents.' The stray cat problem was by now intense. She fed them at considerable expense, while the two sisters subsisted on very much less. Joan's particular worry that day was that in the snow in Scotland some tethered dogs might come to grief. She worried only about animals, not about humans.

Dick Bonham appeared to be ensconced in or behind the house by this time, not unhappily, though with the same concern for the two sisters that he had mentioned at Christmas. An excellent cook, he produced a delicious main course for lunch. The other guest was another regular at the Kappeys' table, Eddie Lloyd, a rather conceited man, I thought, who held a position in the Savill Gardens and related royal anecdotes mainly to prove how much in the know he was.*

The remains of the long correspondence between Dick and Joan survive. There are two postcards from Dick written in June and December 1977 respectively. They are chatty and friendly, and bereft of the rebukes of earlier years. From Yeohampton he wrote:

I had a very satisfactory journey down here – & weather nice & warm & sunny. I am having a dinner party in Caravan tomorrow night. I hope it will go off all right . . . Will be back in Windsor district next week. Dick.

And from Dumfries Dick wrote:

Many thanks for forwarding the 2 Bills! I am still frozen up –

* His favourite story was of a retired housekeeper at Frogmore, a lady of a certain age. One day she curtsied to Queen Mary who congratulated her and then said, 'I wonder if I can still do that.' The two elderly ladies then curtsied in tandem.

& not doing any planting. But Caravan most comfortable & very warm.

I have dinner every evening with the Clark-Maxwells & watch colour TV. Thank you for giving Lewis Dixon-Browne the tel. no. Don't know when I will be returning! Dick.

The cards were perhaps not everything that Joan would have hoped. They were not the cards of a lover. But they must have been warming and Dick's distinctive handwriting, so long awaited over the years, was always welcome. The cards were kept.

Virtually the last letter that Joan wrote to Dick is dated 22 March 1978. The copy she kept began: 'My very dearest Dick . . .' and then it petered out. It had all been said.

By this time Joan was old, seventy-seven in 1978, and Dick himself was nearly sixty-two. Survival on all sides took precedence over romance. There is something both touching and hopeless about Dick's fate as he rallied round in that cat-infested house. Christian was in her room with her china and her paintings, Joan in hers, surrounded by her icon-portraits, and Dick in and out of his caravan, still dressed in his baggy old trousers and tweed jacket.

In my mind I can see them so clearly coming in and out of Joan's front room, each one giving a version of their story to me while the coast was clear – the three of them struggling along together. But it was an unexpected end to the story.

29

The End of the Saga

Christian

The last time I saw Chris a while before she died, I remember being in her room and she was sitting on her sofa opposite me. How sweet and affectionate she looked, somewhat bemused perhaps, with nothing new left to say. But Joan was a hovering presence, disapproving and determined to lure me into her sitting-room. Neither seemed to have a good word for the other, and when I talked to Chris, I felt sure that Joan was listening in.

I did not hear of Christian's death until August 1980. She died on 28 March 1980, a fortnight after Lady Dorothy. I felt great sorrow and also concern at Joan fending for herself, caring for the cats but not for herself.

Christian had dropped down dead and Joan had found her on the scullery floor. At first Joan thought her sister was in a faint, and covered her in rugs and put a cushion under her head. But she was stone dead, alas. Christian was seventy-seven years old. I was told that sadly in her last months Christian had been troubled in the head and believed that Joan was stealing her carpets.

Later I discovered that on the very morning of her death Chris had received a letter from her bank pointing out that her account was overdrawn. The sum in question was less than £100, but I am sure it was beyond Christian's means to repay.* It still makes me shudder to think of her opening that letter on the last day of her life.

When I saw Joan the following September, she was a tiny figure and her grey hair had gone wholly white. She had eleven cats, and told me she would bequeath the house to Dick Bonham and that the cats were to be put to sleep at her death – something often demanded by animal-lovers, but an attitude which I find hard to understand. The theory is that no one will care for the animal as well as its owner. I find this unlikely and it seems selfish.

Joan was left alone, but at least she had Dick Bonham and Betty Worthington and various other kind friends of a wide range of ages – childhood friends who were by then aged eighty, and young Eton boys to help with the garden work, rewarded by tea. At the time I noted in my diary:

> Chris is buried in the Windsor cemetery. So there it is – Major Clough gone years ago – then the funny old Colonel & Francie Kavanagh, Lady Dorothy & Chris herself. A whole little world – and only Joan & Dick left in it . . .

Dick

I was distanced from reliable news of Joan and Dick because Joan no longer used the telephone to reach friends as far away as me, and letter-writing was another occupation of the past. The world had grown smaller and they depended on the more immediate help of close neighbours and friends, of which, fortunately, there were kind examples.

* Christian's bank statement of 19 March 1980 records an overdraft of £37.11.

It was in January 1982 that I saw Joan and heard that Dick had died the year before. He collapsed while driving his car to the Yvonne Arnaud Theatre in Guildford on 1 August 1981 (a few days after the Royal Wedding). He was able to pull up at the roadside, where a passer-by rescued him and drove him to the Royal County Hospital, Guildford. At the hospital he died of a heart attack. There was a post-mortem but no inquest.

It is hard to say what Joan felt. Of course she minded, but when I saw her, she was remarkably calm about it. She never showed any grief to me.

Joan

Joan was to live on until November 1987, Dargai becoming more and more derelict, and overrun by cats. Joan's eyesight dimmed and she was often gravely undernourished through not taking care of herself. Regrettably, there were long periods when I did not see her and times when I even wondered if she was still alive. I remember driving nervously past Dargai and seeing a light on, which gave evidence of habitation, but I had not the courage to go in unannounced.

In no sense was I Joan's guardian, though occasionally I played a small part in her life. In November 1986, about a year before she died, I visited her at Upton House Hospital in Slough, where she was awaiting an operation and refusing to eat. It was one of those depressing places with old ladies dangling over the sides of their chairs. Eventually I found Joan. She recognized me before I recognized her.

I sat with her for some time trying to encourage her to eat. I persuaded her to take a little soup, a sandwich or two and her vitamin, Fortison. In this mission an appeal to her love of the Royal Family came to my aid. 'Now Joan,' I said, 'let's drink a

toast to the Queen . . . Now one to the Duke of Edinburgh.'
She eyed me suspiciously but responded to each challenge. At
times she drifted away from reality, deciding I was a lost lover:
'Now you're here, darling, everything will be all right.' I was
told that her behaviour with the male nursing staff was at
times rather more suggestive and they were quite shocked.

No doubt there were other places where Joan could have
lived in her last days, cleaner, more comfortable, easier to
maintain. It would not be everyone's choice to continue to
struggle on in that large, sad, gloomy house, especially when
the stairs proved too hard to climb and her days and nights
were spent in her uncomfortable front room. It became a kind
of cat sanctuary, overrun with a great number of the species,
some friendly, others distinctly not.

I am glad that Joan was able to spend her last days at
Dargai. It was the home she loved, and she was surrounded by
her icons and her memories. I saw her about a fortnight
before her death at the age of eighty-six, and though she was
frail, her spirit was unvanquished.

Her funeral drew more than a handful of mourners and
her coffin was driven past Dargai in Clarence Road, to be laid
near Chris and Mrs Kappey in Windsor Cemetery.

I continued to wonder what Joan thought about in those last
years. I wondered particularly what she thought about Dick.
Had she gone past the point of minding about him? Possibly,
but probably not.

It is equally easy to dismiss the whole thing as a form of
madness or at least dottiness. I was advised to look into Mun-
chausen's syndrome, which might explain the nature of such
an obsession.

Theirs had been a long-drawn-out drama, exhausting to
both partners in different ways. It was a curious saga, and in

that curious saga there was one element that occurred to me and maybe to Joan also. Dick died and he died unmarried. No one else would get Dick now. Maybe no one entertained that quest, but this was the realm of fantasy. And in the realm of fantasy, Dick was hers for ever.